Jñāna-Yoga
The Way of Knowledge

Jñāna-Yoga
The Way of Knowledge

by

Ramakrishna Puligandla

JAIN PUBLISHING COMPANY
Fremont, California

jainpub.com

Jain Publishing Company, Inc. is a diversified publisher of college textbooks and supplements, as well as professional and scholarly references, and books for the general reader. A complete, up-to-date listing of all the books, with cover images, descriptions, review excerpts, specifications and prices is always available on-line at **jainpub.com**. Our booksPLUS® division provides custom publishing and related services in print as well as electronic formats, and our learn24x7® division offers electronic course and training materials development services.

To

my wife Janaki

with

Love and Gratitude

Foreword

ONE of the most fundamental problems of our times is that of coming to realize the unity underlying the multitude of fragmenting images we have of reality and ourselves. The great tensions within each of us that fracture our being and consume our energies in anxiety and self-doubt, as well as the political tensions in the world that threaten our whole species with extinction, are rooted in our failure to realize that beneath all of these differences is a single, unifying reality. Although the most profound wisdom of both the East and the West has proclaimed this underlying unity, human life has, for the most part, been lived in ignorance of this truth. The reasons we have ignored the deepest truth of our being are many, but they all rest on the assumption that all knowledge is dualistic, that it operates on the level of the subject-object dichotomy. Experience is thought to be impossible unless there is an experiencing subject separate from the objects to be experienced.

The merit of this book is that its author not only recognizes the possibility of a self-revealing non-dual consciousness that grounds all knowledge at the lower, subject-object level, but that he *argues* for his view. Entering into the discussion at the subject-object level, he analyzes the nature of this kind of knowledge, showing that its nature is that of *a construction imposed on reality*, rather than simply a revealing of what is really there. Because all dualistic knowledge is constructed by means of categories imposed on reality by the knower, dualistic knowledge, by itself, never reveals the existence of the deeper, underlying reality. But reflecting on the nature of dualistic knowledge *points to* the presence of something on which knowledge constructions can be imposed.

If dualistic knowledge were the only kind of knowledge possible we could not go beyond the mere possibility of a deeper reality in which it is grounded; what this deeper reality is should remain forever unknown. A kind of phenomenology of consciousness, however, as practised in *yoga*, reveals a consciousness beyond the level of mind and its objects. Stilling the movements of mind, *yoga* enables the deeper reality of unified consciousness to present itself directly, without meditaion, by mind or through mental objects. Although this higher, non-dual, knowledge cannot be described (precisely because it is non-dualistic) it is thoroughly experiential and therefore self-certifying, beyond the possibility of doubt.

In presenting this analysis of ordinary knowledge and the reasons for insisting on a higher, non-dual knowledge, the author helps us re-think not only the nature of human knowledge, but the nature of existence itself. He shows us a deeper ontological foundation of existence, a foundation that reveals communion and coexistence to be more fundamental than differences and strife. Herein we find reasons to use the dualistic knowledge provided by science for higher purposes, to enable us to dwell in the great family of existence in a spirit of compassion, sharing in the life we have in common, the life that grounds all existence. Whether you agree with the author's conclusions or not, his analyses and arguments are sure to stimulate you into deeper thought about the nature and conditions of knowledge and life.

John M. Koller

Preface

JÑĀNA-YOGA, The Way of Knowledge, is an ancient discipline and is one of the four principal paths to knowledge of man and the world and self-knowledge and the realization of ultimate reality. Although self-knowledge and insight into ultimate reality have been pursued by man throughout recorded history, it is in the religio-philosophical traditions of India that the path of knowledge had been systematically formulated and perfected over at least two millennia. The roots of *Jñāna-yoga* are traceable as far back as the *Upaniṣads*; and it is no exaggeration to say that the Upaniṣadic *ṛṣis* — sages, seers, enlightened ones — are among the earliest of *Jñāna-yogins*. Needless to say, the Buddha is a master of the path of knowledge.

Drawing inspiration from the *Upaniṣads* and the *Vedānta-Sūtras* of Bādarāyaṇa, Śaṅkara (AD 7-8), the most renowned Hindu philosopher, poet, mystic, and saint, formulated the central insights of *Jñāna-yoga* into a system known as *Advaita-Vedānta* (non-dualistic *Vedānta*). And Nāgārjuna (AD 1-2), the great Buddhist philosopher and patriarch, inspired by the profound teachings of the Buddha, in particular the Doctrine of Dependent Origination, expressed the fundamental insights of *Jñāna-yoga* in his celebrated works which form the foundation of *Mādhyamaka* Buddhism (The Middle Way). The most famous of these works is the *Mūla-madhyamaka-kārikā*.

The present work is based upon the teachings of these two *Jñāna-yogins*. I have studied their teachings both from theoretical and experimental standpoints for over three decades now; accordingly, this book represents my own study, reflection, and practice.

What is the reason for my writing this book? The main reason is that, although there are many works, both major and minor, on the other three paths as well as on *Advaita-Vedānta* and *Mādhyamaka* Buddhism, there are few works which deal with the fundamental insights of *Jñāna-yoga* as such. It is thus the chief objective of this book to clearly present and discuss what I construe to be the essential insights of *Jñāna-yoga*, which may be expressed as the following three principles: the Principle of Superimposition, the Principle of Dependent Origination, and the Principle of Two Truths. I have endeavoured to state these principles in a clear and straightforward manner and systematically discuss their significance as well as that of their consequences. And in order to facilitate understanding on the part of Western readers, I have employed, wherever beneficial and appropriate, the concepts and terminology of the Western philosophical tradition — for example, categorial framework, analytic truth, contingent truth, necessary truth; in addition, I have drawn upon modern science to illustrate some of the concepts and ideas of *Jñāna-yoga*. And in order to familiarize the reader with the terminology of *Jñāna-yoga*, I have supplied in parentheses Sanskrit terms.

Jñāna-yoga, unlike many other philosophies, is not a merely logico-analytic or speculative inquiry which has no bearing upon our lives and experience. On the contrary, *Jñāna-yoga* includes in itself as an integral component experimental investigation, many methods and procedures of which are drawn from *Rāja-yoga*, the *yoga* of psycho-physiological investigation. In other words, the theoretical — logico-analytic — part of *Jñāna-yoga* is based upon certain indubitable facts of our experience, our modes of being. For this reason, certain claims of *Jñāna-yoga* can only be certified through experimental inquiry. That is, for *Jñana-yoga*, mere internal consistency is not enough; in addition, the inquiry should be securely grounded in our experiential base. Although the experimental part of *Jñāna-yoga* has no counterpart in the Western tradition, it shares certain methods and goals with phenomenology, a contemporary Western school of philosophy, founded by the German thinker Edmund Husserl, at the turn of the century. I shall therefore briefly explicate the notion of phenomenology.

Simply put, phenomenology, as a method of philosophic inquiry, consists of systematic investigation of the variety of modes of human consciousness. That is, a phenomenologist is one who carefully studies and faithfully describes the various states of human consciousness. What does it mean to describe a state of consciousness? To describe a state of consciousness is to describe the contents of consciousness — objects of consciousness — faithfully and in a detailed manner. Anything may be an object of consciousness, a so-called physical object, an emotion, a thought, an idea, a mental image, a dream, a hallucination, and so on. That is, insofar as phenomenological inquiry is concerned, anything, whether called 'physical' or 'psychological', can be an object of consciousness. The purpose of phenomenological investigation, then, is to provide a catalog of descriptions of the various states of human consciousness; such a catalog is indeed the phenomenological data, which serve as the basis for analytic inquiry.

When someone makes a claim about a certain state of consciousness, he should tell us as to how he came to make the claim and what one is to do in order to determine the truth or falsity of the claim. It is in this manner that phenomenological investigation is essential for the pursuit of *Jñāna-yoga*. Let me illustrate this point. Suppose that someone claimed that there is a state of consciousness without objects, and another countered by saying that there is no such state, because it is simply impossible. How is one to settle this dispute which concerns an extremely significant point? Mere definitional arguments, no matter how meticulous and elegant, are of no avail here; what is needed is a procedure by which to determine the truth or falsity of the claim and thereby settle the dispute. It is worth emphasizing that the thinker who denies the existence of objectless consciousness should also tell us how he came to know that such a state of consciousness is impossible and therefore does not and cannot exist. If neither party is able to provide us with any experimental procedure by which to determine the truth of his claim, we are entitled to reject both claims as dogmatic and groundless, and the fact remains that one of the two claims must be true and the other must be false; and any serious inquirer will look for methods or devise some to determine the truth or falsity of the claims.

It is thus clear that phenomenological investigation is part and parcel of *Jñāna-yoga*. At this point, it is to be noted that, although we have described the experimental procedures of *Jñāna-yoga* as 'phenomenology', phenomenology as done in the West is elementary compared to *Rāja-yoga*, the source of various techniques of *Jñāna-yoga*. It is most unfortunate and disappointing that Western phenomenology is almost exclusively talk with little or no actual phenomenological investigation. In keen contrast, *Rāja-yoga* is an extraordinarily rich phenomenological discipline, in that it investigates not only the various states of consciousness that form the bulk of our everyday life, but also formulates methods and procedures by which to bring about specific states of consciousness far from the ordinary and everyday. Such procedures enable us to bring about states of consciousness in a controlled fashion, and controlled experimentation is at the heart of all rational-scientific inquiry. And insofar as *Jñāna-yoga* employs the experimental techniques of *Rāja-yoga*, in conjunction with rigorous logico-analytic inquiry, *Jñāna-yoga* is unquestionably rational and scientific.

Now to the inevitable question: Is *Jñāna-yoga* mysticism? Is there anything mystical about *Jñāna-yoga*? It is common knowledge that the terms 'mysticism' and 'mystical' are notoriously ambiguous and mean almost anything one wants. Nevertheless, there is a core meaning of 'mysticism', acknowledged by various scholars as a result of systematic and detailed study of the writings of mystics of different times and climes. The core meaning may be expressed as follows: A mystic is one who has attained insight into ultimate reality, by realizing his identity with ultimate reality. This insight results in his feeling at one with all existence; in a word, the mystic sees himself in everything and all things in himself. That is, the mystic is wholly free of every form of alienation and is fully at home with the world. The sense of oneness with reality — at-one-ment — which transcends space and time and the senses and intellect, which defies all descriptions, names and forms, is the hallmark of mysticism, East or West. *Jñāna-yoga* is mysticism in the sense of the core meaning of 'mysticism'. Let it be immediately noted that it has, however, nothing to do with mysticism in the usual derogatory sense of rabid romanticism, incurable irrationalism, titillation with the occult, and cultic preoccupations. Quite the contrary, *Jñāna-yoga* is mysticism thoroughly grounded in relentless rationality. It is worth emphasizing also that *Jñāna-yoga* is *not* a religion undedrstood as theism. Thoroughgoing atheism — lack of belief in a God who is the creator, protector, and destroyer of the world — is fully compatible with *Jñāna-yoga*; for, according to *Jñāna-yoga*, the plethora of Gods one encounters in various religions, past, present, and future, are all no more and no less than products of our own intellect and emotions. This is not to say, however, that such Gods are unreal in the sense in which a square-circle or the son of a barren woman is unreal; rather, all these Gods are phenomenally real — that is, they have a categorial, mento-emotional reality; but they are not to be mistaken, either singly or collectively, for ultimate reality, the realization of which alone is the supreme goal of *Jñāna-yoga*.

I shall bring this preface to a close with a few remarks on the two kinds of knowledge and truth, a detailed discussion of which is undertaken in connection with the Principle of Two Truths. The two kinds of knowledge and truth are as follows: the lower, relative, conditioned, dependent, phenomenal, perceptual-conceptual (categorial) truth (*saṁvṛtti-satya*) and the higher, unconditioned, direct, immediate, intuitive, non-perceptual-non-conceptual (non-categorial) truth (*paramārtha-satya*). According to *Jñāna-yoga*, the lower truth is non-soteriological, while the higher truth is soteriological. What is meant by 'soteriological'? Soteriological knowledge is knowledge that has the power to radically transform the human being. We are all well aware that man, as he exists, is a tragic spectacle — he is ignorant, greedy, cruel, alienated, suffers from fear, angst, existential disquietudes, and various forms of ill-being, his greatest fear being death; and there is no need to recount the litany of horrors that is human history; and now man has arrived at a point where he could simply destory the entire planet at lightning speed. And it is the supreme irony that man has acquired the power to devastate the world through knowledge which he has himself painstakingly produced. What went wrong? The answer, according to *Jñāna-yoga*, is plain and clear: lower knowledge and truth, no matter how impeccable and efficacious in its own domain , is bereft of the power to transform man; in a word, lower knowledge is non-soteriological; but man mistakenly believes that he could transform himself through the acquisition and accummulation of lower knowledge and truth. Simply look around, and you will find human beings highly accomplished in some department or other of lower knowledge, but they are not exempt from the ailments that bedevil the ordinary, unlettered people; that is, they suffer from jealousy, anger, greed, cruelty, and fear of death itself. That someone is a distinguished mathematician, zoologist, logician, physicist, philosopher, computer-scientist, psychologist, etc. does not mean that he is free from ignorance, pain, and suffering. This fact in itself is resounding testimony to the claim of *Jñāna-yoga* that lower knowledge is devoid of the power to radically transform the human being. Only the higher knowledge and truth are soteriological, in that they transform the human being into a sane, healthy, joyful, fearless, peaceful, and wise being. And for this reason, the way of attaining the higher truth is at the very heart of *Jñāna-yoga*. Hence *Jñāna-yoga*, The Way of Knowledge, is a path to enlightenment.

It is to be noted that *Jñāna-yoga* is not suitable for all people; it serves best those who by inclination and ability are of an inquiring bent; it is for people who will not accept any claim without systematic investigation and certification. Things which others may readily accept, the follower of the path of knowledge will not. The point, then, is that other paths may serve certain types of people better and more efficaciously; and, when followed earnestly, diligently, and patiently, these paths, too, transform the human being.

The present work is therefore for all those who wish to pursue *Jñāna-yoga*, either by itself or as part of another path. It is my humble hope that the reader will find this work of some help and assistance in his own quest for the knowledge of ultimate reality. And if this book contributes even in a small measure to this end, I will have been more than justified and rewarded in writing it.

The readers may note that the terms 'man', 'he' and 'his' are to be understood as referring to the human being in general, irrespective of gender.

R. Puligandla

Contents

Acknowledgments

I wish to thank my former students, Mr. Mark MacDowell and Mr. Donald Matesz, for their perusal of the manuscript and for their perceptive comments. I am indebted to my friend, Professor Robert L. Greenwood, of the University of South Alabama, for his constructive criticisms and helpful suggestions. And I am most grateful to Professor John M. Koller, of Rensselaer Polytechnic Institute, for deeming this work worthy of his foreword.

I am thankful to the authorities of the University of Toledo for a grant toward research assistance, and to Ms. Kathleen Skurzewski for her meticulous and elegant preparation of the manuscript and for her patience with scholarly idiosyncrasies.

Any faults that may yet remain are, of course, entirely my own.

Ramakrishna Puligandla

1

Introduction
An Outline of the Four Paths

THE concept of *Jñāna-yoga*, as such, comes to us from the philosophical and religious traditions of India. According to these traditions, there are four principal paths — ways, methods — leading to the attainment of insight into and experience of ultimate reality, variously called *Brahman, Ātman,* 'The That', *Nirvāṇa, Śūnyatā* (Void, Emptiness), *Tathatā* (Thusness, Suchness), and so on. The four paths are: *Bhakti-yoga, Karma-yoga, Jñāna-yoga,* and *Rāja-yoga.* In the present context, the term *yoga* may simply be understood as path, way, and method. It is to be noted that the Indian tradition, unlike almost all others, emphasizes that, insofar as human beings differ from each other, different types of persons find different paths appropriate and efficacious to them. Thus each of the above paths is best suited to human beings of a certain type. To prescribe a single path to all people is like a physician's prescribing one and the same medicine to people suffering from different kinds of ailment and disease. The result of such a single prescription, whatever it may be and however kindly dispensed, is positively harmful; for, besides not curing the person, it creates complications which may and often do lead to death. Some people might object to the claim that human beings differ from each other by saying that it is undemocratic, elitist, provincial, and even racist. I should at once point out that such an objection is not based on any facts but is merely the reaction of blind and uncritical commitment to a mistaken conception of egalitarianism. What is the mistaken conception of egalitarianism I speak of? Genuine egalitarianism is based, paradoxical as it might seem, on the recognition of the fact that human beings are different from each other. The true spirit of egalitarianism may be expressed as follows: human beings are, as a matter of fact, different from one another but this fact should not be taken as justification for treating certain persons and peoples disrespectfully, inconsiderately, and inhumanely; on the contrary, despite their differences, which are many and varied, all human beings, simply by virtue of the fact that they are human beings, are entitled to equality of respect, dignity, consideration, opportunity, and to equality before the law. The heart of true and authentic egalitarianism, then, is this commitment toward all human beings, irrespective of their differences, but not the denial of their differences, whatever the reasons for the differences. It is the denial of the differences that I call "mistaken conception of egalitarianism". It is clear that the recognition of differences among human beings is presupposed by true egalitarianism. For is it not the case that there would be no need for egalitarianism were all human beings equal, much as the products emerging from the assembly line? To put it differently, where there are no differences there is no need for egalitarianism.

It is an undeniable fact of observation that human beings differ from one another in many respects — physical, mental, and emotional — whatever the reasons for the differences. Thus some people are predominantly intellectual, reflective, and contemplative; others emotional (feeling-oriented), aesthetic, and artistic; yet others mechanically inclined and pragmatic; still others religious, and so on. For our purposes, the reasons as to why human beings are different from each other are irrelevant. That is, we start out by simply acknowledging the fact that human beings are different from one another and then ask, in light of this fact, whether it makes sense to think that there is a single path for all human beings. The answer is clearly in the negative. Thus consider, as an example, the following case: a man wants to go from New York to San Francisco. Suppose we gave him the map of an air-route. This map will serve him well only if he has an airplane. But if he has only an automobile, is it not appropriate that we suply him with a road-map? On the other hand, if he has a yacht and wishes to travel by it, neither of the earlier maps will be useful to him; instead he needs the map of a water-route. Just as people with different modes of transportation need different kinds of maps, so also human beings with different physical-mental-emotional makeup need different routes — paths — for the knowledge and experience of ultimate reality. Hence different paths.

As its title indicates, this book is concerned with *Jñāna-yoga*, the path of knowledge. Its aim is to set forth in a clear and uncomplicated manner the fundamentals of *Jñāna-yoga*. I am aware that *Jñāna-yoga* is a vast subject and had been through the ages inquired into from different standpoints by different thinkers, and consequently there exists on this subject a large number of works, ancient, modern, and contemporary. However, it is not my purpose in this book to offer a historical treatment of *Jñāna-yoga*; rather, as has already been stated, the chief objective of the book is to present the essentials of *Jñāna-yoga*, needless to mention, in light of my own inquiry, understanding, and experience. I shall now turn to a brief description of the four paths.

(a) *Bhakti-yoga* (the path of devotion): This path is most suited to those people who are predominantly of a devotional turn of personality. These are people who are not much concerned with intellectual inquiry; rather, they are persons capable of unshakable faith in and devotion to God (of course in their chosen form). Cultivation of humility, love, charity, non-aggression, constant remembrance of God, and absolute and unqualified self-surrender to God are the heart of this path. Through self-surrender to God, the devotee (*bhakta*) eventually succeeds in emptying the ego and on such emptying arise direct knowledge and experience of God. It is a common error among the more cerebral people to think that the path of devotion is an easy path. Nothing, however, could be farther from the truth. The path of devotion, as explained here, is as arduous and

demanding as any of other three paths. In order to appreciate
how difficult this path is, simply think of what the path demands:
freedom from the assaults of doubt (concerning the existence of
God), complete submission to Him, constant rememberance of
God, and thereby emptying the ego — killing the ego. To the
devotee, the existence of God is not a matter of mere belief or
intellectual demonstration; instead, for him, if anything is
certain, and absolutely certain, it is the existence of God, the
Lord and Master of all existence. Further, for the devotee, in
light of his total surrender to God, everything that happens
because it is pleasing to God: "Who am I to complain? Who am
I to tell Him I am hungry and in need of food? Does He not know?
Is there anything that is hidden from Him? Food comes to me
when He, the Lord, is pleased; if it pleases Him that I go without
food, I go without food but I am nobody to gripe and grumble."
This is not to say, however, that one who treads the path of
devotion should not work and make an honest living. The point
is rather that for the devotee his efforts and their successes as
well as failures are all God's will and pleasure. Thus he does not
feel proud and boastful when he is successful and prosperous or
feel frustrated and blame others or God when he fails. For the
devotee, he is himself a nobody, a nothing, while God is everything,
the Lord of all that happens and does not happen. It is to be
stressed that his attitude on the part of the devotee is not to be
confused with fatalism; for at the very core of the devotional
path there is God, who is to be served with utter devotion;
consequently, there is no room in this path for hopelessness,
anguish, nihilism, etc. since the devotee is fully anchored in
God. There is no such anchoring to the fatalist and he is
therefore open to the onslaughts of doubt, despair, nihilism, and
hopelessness. The devotee is ever free, peaceful, loving, humble,
and joyful; for he has placed himself in the hands of the most
high, whom none can touch but who touches everything. It
should be clear by now that the devotional path is as hard and
exacting as any other. If you are still unconvinced, try to attain
freedom from doubt and cultivate humility and surrender
yourself absolutely and unconditionally to God, and you will see
how tough the devotional path is.

(b) *Karma-yoga* (the path of action): This path is best suited for those people who are essentially of an active nature — the doers. That is, it serves best those who are predominantly activity-oriented, in contrast with, for example, those who are relatively passive, reflective, and contemplative. The path of action, then, is for those who, through their committed and active involvement in the affairs of the world, seek to attain the knowledge and experience of ultimate reality. Thus at the heart of the path of action lie total commitment and dedication to actively working for the betterment of mankind. We need to clarify here the term 'action'. 'Action' in the context of *Karma-yoga* means action without attachment (*niṣkāma-karma*). Only actions thus performed — without attachment — constitute *Karma-yoga*. Actions performed with attachment are grounded in ignorance and unfreedom. And since the goal of *Karma-yoga*, like that of the other three *yoga*s, is knowledge, wisdom, peace, and freedom, actions performed with attachment are incompatible with *Karma-yoga*. The underlying insight here is that attachment is born of egoism, of one form or another; therfore, actions done with attachment are selfishly motivated actions, no matter how subtly veiled is such motivation. It is only actions purified of every vestige of selfishness that are truly actions without attachment. One performs actions which, in light of one's best knowledge and belief, are appropriate under a given set of circumstances but is not concerned with the success or failure of the actions or the fruits thereof; for to be so concerned is precisely what it is to be attached. It is of the utmost importance to note that it is not performing or not performing an action that is the cause of pain, sorrow, and suffering; rather, it is the attitude one has toward the consequences (fruits) of acting or not acting. Thus if a student studies a subject well — with the aim of attaining understanding and mastery — and takes an examination and for some reason does not do well and receives only a moderate grade and feels bad about it, it is clear that his pain and unhappiness are brought about by his attitude toward the *results* (fruits) of his taking the examination, but not by his taking the examination. *Karma-yoga* exhorts men to perform actions to the best of their abilities and facilities and not grieve over the consequences of the actions. When a person is ill and suffering great pain, *Karma-yoga* requires that we spare no effort at our disposal to alleviate his suffering and restore his health. But, despite our best efforts, if the person dies, for us to feel bad and cry and lament is clearly a mark of ignorance, unwisdom, and unfreedom; for if we honestly examine ourselves it becomes clear that we grieve because there is somewhere subtly hidden some attachment, which in the last analysis is but a form of selfishness. *Karma-yoga* demands that men do their best and not be attached to and thereby be perturbed by the consequences of their actions. It is worth emphasizing that the actions are always to be unselfishly motivated and performed for the enhancement of the well-being of all sentient beings, individually and collectively. Action without attachment, then, is action untained by selfishness and egoism. Great social and political reformers and others who unremittingly work for the betterment of the world are *Karma-yogins* in varying degrees. The follower of the path of action is further exhorted to dedicate everyone of his actions as an offering to God (in his chosen form). Now ask: What kind of things does one offer God? Is it not true that only the best at one's disposal is worthy of offering to God? What is meant by 'best' here? By 'best' is meant everything pure and of the highest value. It is clear that every action the follower of *Karma-yoga* performs must be pure — in the sense of unselfish, non-egoistic, and unattached — in order for it to qualify to be a fitting offering to God.

One might ask now: does it mean, then, that the follower of the path of action must be a theist? No, it means nothing of the kind. If one is a theist, one's actions are looked upon as offerings to God; but the emphasis here is on non-attachment and purity of action, not on one's being a theist or atheist. That one is an avowed atheist does not mean that one cannot perform action without attachment. The main thrust of *Karma-yoga* is that through dedication to serving man by pure, unselfish, and unattached action even the atheist eventually gains insight into ultimate reality. We may note again that *Karma-yoga*, like *Bhakti-yoga*, is aimed at emptying the ego in order that one may experience ultimate reality; that is, the goal is the same and only the paths are different, each being appropriate and best suited to persons of a certain type. The *Bhakti-yogin* succeeds in emptying the ego through unswerving and absolute self-surrender to God, whereas the *Karma-yogin* accomplishes this same goal by cultivating utter unselfishness and by working through action without attachment for the welfare of all sentient beings. In either case, the destination is the same: experience of ultimate reality through seeing the emptiness of the ego.

It should be clear that *Karma-yoga*, like *Bhakti-yoga*, is an arduous and exacting path. If someone doubts this claim, let him strive to be unselfish and unattached and be maximally concerned for the well-being of all; he will soon see that the path of action is as difficult and demanding as any other.

(c) *Rāja-yoga* (the path of psycho-physiological exploration): This path is eminently suited to those people who have the inclination and ability for a long, detailed, and systematic investigation of the physiological and psychological strands of their personalities. It goes without saying that this path requires great effort and concentration. *Rāja-yoga* consists of a variety of psycho-physiological exercises and techniques, by practising which one gains knowledge and control of the physiological and psychological processes — knowledge and control of the physical, emotional, and mental aspects of one's being. Patañjali's *Yoga-Sūtras* is the classic text on *Rāja-yoga*, also called the *Aṣṭāṅga-yoga*, meaning the eight-limbed *yoga*. There are, in addition, innumerable works of major and minor significance on the subject. The aim of *Rāja-yoga*, like that of *Bhakti-yoga* and *Karma-yoga*, is knowledge and experience of ultimate reality. *Rāja-yoga* realizes this aim through experimental inquiry into the psycho-physiological makeup of the human being. For this reason, *Rāja-yoga* is aptly described as the science *par excellence* of man. Systematic observation of different states of consciousness, ordinary as well as extraordinary, is the warp and woof of *Rāja-yoga*. From the total cessation of mental activity — *cittavṛtti-nirodha* — arises the experience of ultimate reality. An accomplished *Rāja-yogin* is one who had acquired such power and control over the mind.

Experimenting with various powerful techniques such as breath-control (*prāṇāyāma*), the practitioner of *Rāja-yoga* comes to command knowledge of the various facets of the constitution of man. He also gains knowledge of the subconscious and the unconscious and thereby of the modes of being and operations of the physical, emotional, and mental domains. Through complete mastery and control of mind, the *Rāja-yogin* comes to see the emptiness of the ego and thereby gains knowledge and experience of ultimate reality.

It may be noted again that the emptying of the ego — what is the same, clearly seeing that the ego is empty — is central to *Rāja-yoga*, as it is to *Bhakti-yoga* and *Karma-yoga*, although their methods are different. The *Rāja-yogin* sees the emptiness of the ego by disciplined work on himself. In order to see how difficult and demanding is *Rāja-yoga*, one need only realize the chattering that incessantly goes on in one's own mind without one's being even aware of it; and if one is not aware of and not in charge of one's own thoughts and feelings, in what sense can one claim to be free? Thoughts and emotions are always arising apparently without being initiated and set into motion by oneself. The main point of *Rāja-yoga*, then, is that as long as one exists in this manner, one is both ignorant and unfree. But when by effort and discipline the modifications of the mind are brought to a total cessation, ultime reality is revealed — just as the reflection of say, the moon, is clearly seen in calm and unruffled lake.

(d) *Jñāna-yoga* (the path of knowledge): I shall present here only a brief and general account of *Jñāna-yoga*, a detailed treatment of which will be taken up in the chapters to come. The path of knowledge is for those persons who are distinguished by an inquiring turn of mind. That is, this path is for those who by temperament, ability, and training are inclined toward and most seriously committed to rational inquiry of the highest standards into man, the world, and ultimate reality. Highly developed logical-analytical intellect, coupled with the facility for keen observation and flashes of synthetic intuition — the ability to see several things or aspects of things as constituting a consistent, significant, and illuminating pattern — are essential for *Jñāna-yoga*. *Jñāna-yoga* is therefore for those who accept no claim unless and until every objection against it has been successfully answered and every doubt allayed. Thus whereas the follower of *Bhakti-yoga* quells all doubts by cultivating unshakable faith in and devotion to God, the follower of *Jñāna-yoga* overcomes doubt through the development and exercise of discriminative intellect (*buddhi*). For the practitioner of *Jñāna-yoga*, then, mind and its activities — production of doubt and knowledge — are themselves the object of relentless scrutiny and understanding. It is by attaining such understanding through rigorous and uncompromising inquiry that the follower of *Jñāna-yoga* is led to the knowledge and experience of ultimate reality. It is obvious that *Jñāna-yoga* is not for the intellectually weak, timid, and lazy; rather, it is for those whose personalities are predominantly cerebral and whose commitment to rational inquiry is absolute and unqualified. In other words, the follower of *Jñāna-yoga* is one endowed with extraordinary intellectual energy and a natural bent for reflection and contemplation.

Like the other three paths, *Jñāna-yoga* is a difficult and exacting path. It is true that there are many who hold in contempt persons given to intellectual inquiry in the sense of *Jñāna-yoga*. This negative attitude is understandable once we realize how many people find it difficult and painful to clearly think, understand, and express themselves. Just find out for yourself how rarely we really listen to someone speak. Seldom do we hear with attention, let alone understand, what the other person is saying. It is only occasionally, as interruptions of the stream of our own thoughts and emotions, that we happen to listen to someone speak. What this means, then, is that undivided attention, clarity of thought and expression, and unbiased and systematic inquiry are the heartbeat of *Jñāna-yoga*.

It is through unrelenting inquiry, sustained reflection, and serene contemplation that the follower of *Jñāna-yoga* is led to the knowledge of the emptiness of the ego. Seeing the emptiness of the ego is thus the goal common to all the paths; and the *Jñāna-yogin* attains this goal primarily through the instrumentality of discriminative intellect. On comprehending the emptiness of the ego, there arises the knowledge and experience of ultimate reality.

It is worth noting that although the four paths are clearly distinguishable through their salient features, it would be a mistake to think that they are therefore mutually exclusive. On the contrary, it is often the case that one and the same person practises more than one path, one of them being dominant and most suited to him. Thus any of the four paths may be primary with another as secondary, depending upon the person's temperament and inclination. It is only rarely that one pursues one of the paths to the exclusion of the others.

I shall conclude this introduction with some examples of the different types of *yogins*. The prophets of the Old Testament, Jesus, and the apostles of the New Testament are exclusively *Bhakti-yogins*; Augustine, Aquinas, and Meister Eckhart are primarily *Bhakti-yogins* and secondarily *Jñāna-yogins*; Gandhi, Mother Teresa, and Martin Luther King are exemplars of the combination of *Bhakti* and *Karma* paths; Plato and Plotinus are primarily *Jñāna-yogins*; Śaṅkara, the great *Advaita-Vedāntin*, and Nāgārjuna, the celebrated Buddhist philosopher and patriarch, are exclusively *Jñāna-yogins*; and so on.

It cannot be overemphasized that for a person to follow a path not suited to him is not only not beneficial but is even harmful to him. Thus it is of the first importance to find out what path(s) is most appropriate to oneself. Think of someone, in whom strength and courage are not dominant traits, trying to become a great warrior; before long, he will surely lose his life.

2

The Essentials of Jñāna-Yoga

IN the previous chapter, I briefly presented the four paths, one of which is that of knowledge (*Jñāna-yoga*), the subject of this book. In the present chapter, I shall undertake a detailed and systematic presentation of the fundamental insights and practice of *Jñāna-yoga*. The term *jñāna* means knowledge; accordingly, I shall begin with a clarification of the concept of knowledge.

If *jñāna* means knowledge, one might ask, is not everyone engaged in the pursuit of knowledge a practitioner of *Jñāna-yoga*? The answer to this question requires us to distinguish the various senses of the term 'knowledge' and explicitly state in which of the senses pursuit of knowledge is to be regarded as *Jñāna-yoga*.

A seminal insight of *Jñāna-yoga* is that all knowledge that is expressible and hence communicable is governed by a fundamental dualism: the knower and the known; which may more generally be expressed as the dualism of the self and the other. What this means is that the very concept of knowledge implies a knower and an object of knowledge. This in turn means that expressible and communicable knowledge cannot be produced by abolishing the distinction between the knower and the known.

It is further implied by this fundamental dualism of the knower and the known that the domain of the knowable is one of plurality. What do I mean by this? The known, insofar as it is known as an object — of whatever kind, physical or psychological — can only be known as one among many. That is, knowing necessarily requires distinguishing (one from another). Where it is not possible to so distinguish, knowledge expressible and communicable is impossible. To put it somewhat dramatically, if there were only one object in the üniverse it could not be known to be an *object*, although it could certainly be known as the *other,* this latter knowing being based on none other than the primordial distinction of self and the other, the knower and the known. To put it differently, where there is no plurality of objects there can be no knowing an *object,* either. Thus it is clear that the entire domain of the knowable consists of variety and multiplicity of objects. In brief, all expressible and communicable knowledge is confined to the realm of the many and varied. This realm is collectively referred to as "the phenomenal world". This is to say that all expressible and communicable knowledge · is necessarily of some phenomenon or other.

We shall now clarify the concept of knowledge by distinguishing three levels. Leve 1: Consists of knowledge of objects — phenomena — constituting a certain domain; for example, physics, and the various specialities within physics, such as astronomy, low-temperature physics, nuclear physics, and so on; or biology and the many specialities therein. Level 2: consists of knowledge of the foundations of a given discipline (at Level 1), foundations in the sense that they support the discipline and lend to the discipline its specific form, content, and character. The foundations of any discipline at Level 1 may be referred to as "categorial framework" as well as "perceptual-conceptual framework". Someone may be a physicist in the sense of one who investigates some subset(s) of phenomena constituting the domain of physics; but he may not have inquired into the foundations of his own discipline and therefore may either be wholly unaware of its foundations or only have some vague and unclear notions about them. Most scientists, including some very successful ones, are of this kind. This remark is not to be construed as an accusation but merely as a statement of fact. However, it is often the case that only those scientists who also inquire into the foundations of their disciplines make original and radical contributions to the advancement of their fields — for example, Galileo, Newton, Darwin, Einstein, Schrödinger, Heisenberg, to mention only a few of the truly great scientists. Level 3: Goes beyond knowledge of particular categorial frameworks underlying particular disciplines to knowledge of the nature of categorial frameworks in general and thereby of the nature of knowledge producible by categorial frameworks. Knowledge based on categorial frameworks may simply be called "categorial knowledge". Level 3 knowledge, then, is knowledge concerning the nature of all categorial knowledge — of categorial knowledge in general.

A moment's reflection reveals that the transition from Level 1 to Level 3 is in the direction of increasing abstraction and generality; knowledge of particular objects of a certain kind, knowledge of the foundations (the categorial framework) on which rests the knowledge of particular objects of a certain kind, and knowledge of the nature of categorial frameworks in general and hence of the nature of all categorial knowledge. *Jñāna-yoga*, understood as the path of knowledge, is knowledge of Level 3. Only he who pursues knowledge in the sense of Level 3 can correctly be said to be a practitioner of *Jñāna-yoga*, the path of knowledge. It is to be emphasized that the pursuit of knowledge at a certain level does not exclude the pursuit of knowledge at the other levels. Thus one may be a physicist and thus produce knowledge of particular objects of a certain type; and he may also inquire into knowledge at Level 2, and Level 3. That is, there is nothing in or about *Jñāna-yoga* that would require one to belittle, denigrate, or exclude the pursuit of knowledge at Levels 1 and 2. It is worth emphasizing, however, that unless and until one embarks on inquiry at Level 3 one cannot be said to be a follower of the path of knowledge.

What is a categorial framework? The notion of categorial framework stems from a central insight of *Jñāna-yoga*, namely, the kind of knowledge a certain kind of beings are capable of producing is inextricably bound up with their psycho-psychological makeup. This means, first, that among various kinds of beings human beings constitute only one; and second, the nature and limits of human knowledge is governed by the physiological and psychological constitution of the human being. This is the same as saying that had human beings been of a different psycho-physiological makeup than their present one, the nature and limits of the knowledge they produce would be different (from that which they now, as a matter of fact, produce). There should be nothing surprising about this claim; for simply imagine our optic nerves being arranged differently; then it is only to be expected that our experience of colours would have been different from our present experience of them. Similar is the case with regard to our other sense-organs. It is obvious, then, that our perceptions are ineluctably bound up with the constitution of our perceptual apparatus. To take another example, we are the kind of beings who cannot see the back of an object simultaneously with the front. That is, if I hold up an object, say a book, in front of you, you can only see its front but not its back. There is nothing mysterious about this observation; on the contrary, it is a correct report about our ways of perceiving. We also know that changes in our bio-chemical makeup result in changes in our perceptions. It is a fact, then, that our knowledge is a function of our physiological constitution. Our claims as to what sorts of things makeup the world and what properties they possess, and what relations obtain among them is a function of our psysiological makeup.

But in addition to our physiological makeup, our psychological constitution determines the nature of the knowledge we produce. The term 'psychological' is to be understood here as encompassing the mental and the emotional. In short, the psychological consists of the sentient and sapient, the emotional and the mental, respectively. What comes to us through our sense-organs is ordered and organized — categorized — according to our psychological constitution. It goes without saying that beings endowed with a different psychological constitution than we are will organize and categorize differently what they receive through their sense-organs, thereby resulting in knowledge-claims different from ours. It is to be noted that our psychological makeup allows for a variety of ways of organizing and categorizing, each way being appropriate to a certain end and purpose. All the possible different ways of ordering, organizing, and categorizing that which comes through our sensory channels and equipment define the range of our psychological makeup.

A categorial framework, then, broadly speaking, defines a certain way of arranging and ordering— categorizing — the sensory input through our perceptual endowment, thereby leading to our claims as to what the world is like. To the question as to whether all perceptions are the result of sensory input from what we normally call "an external origin" or whether there are also internal perceptions (perceptions whose sources are within), for example, dream and imagination, the answer is straightforward; yes, there are external perceptions — seeing a tree in the yard — and internal perceptions — dreaming and imagining — and these two kinds of perception are clearly distinguishable; and, as a matter of fact, we all so distinguish them. And the important point here is that perceptions, whether external or internal, are all organized and ordered according to a given categorial framework.

To articulate a categorial framework is to state the fundamental principles and the various categories and the ordering rules which constitute the categorial framework. I shall not go here into a detailed discussion of any particular categorial framework; rather, I shall illustrate some of the ideas seminal to the notion of a categorial framework; for, after all, it is not my purpose here to propose a certain categorial framework but only to enable the reader to gain an understanding and appreciation of the idea of categorial framework in general.

Take, for instance, the distinction between the physical and the mental. Insofar as this distinction is given to us directly in our experience and therefore incontrovertible, to regard the distinction as basic to our knowledge-enterprise is to regard 'physical' and 'mental' as two categories. Thus to acknowledge this distinction is to enunciate a fundamental principle of the categorial framework: all acceptable knowledge-claims must be in accord with the physical-mental distinction.

Consider the concept of causation. To hold that no event can occur without a cause(s) is to regard 'cause' and 'effect' as categories in a certain framework. It is thus an essential principle of the categorial framework that no event can occur without a cause(s) and no claim to knowledge which violates this principle can be accepted.

To take another example, the categories 'substance' and 'attribute' are to be found in many frameworks; 'substance' refers to the thing as such, the underlying substratum, and 'atribute' to the properties (qualities) possessed by the thing. Thus to say that this apple is red is to attribute the property of redness to a thing called 'apple'. It is of course immediately granted that the substance (substratum) is not given to the senses but only the qualities. 'Substance' and 'attribute', understood in this manner, are categories of the framework.

Let us now briefly consider the subject of space and time. A given thinker may regard 'space' and 'time' as categories, in the sense that they are fundamental to and underlie all our experience. Thus everything we perceive as external is located in space *and* time — is somewhere and somewhen. In contrast, everything we percieve as internal, such as thoughts and feelings, is not locatable in space, at least in the kind of space in which we claim are located such things as chairs, stones, etc. — the bird was in the cage in the livingroom this morning before I left home. Thoughts and feelings are only in time but not in space. And the thinker may further regard space and time as existing independently and absolutely (non-relatively). Such is the case with the categorial framework underlying the physics constructed by Newton. However, another thinker, such as Einstein, may hold and even try to provide evidence for the view that space and time are relative and, more importantly, neither space nor time exists but only the space-time continuum. These two frameworks illustrate the fact that two or more frameworks may have some categories in common, although at the theoretic level the categories may be assigned different significance in the frameworks. Thus it is fully permissible and perfectly sensible in both the Newtonian and Einsteinian frameworks to claim that we experience objects such as trees and rocks as being in space and time, leaving aside the whole question concerning the mode and manner of existence of space and time and whether or not they are relative, absolute, dependent, independent, and so on. This is precisely what I mean by saying that the categories of space and t me have a common experiential basis in both the Newtonian and Einsteinian frameworks but are understood differently at the theoretical level. Needless to say, such differences become explicit in a detailed exhibition of the categorial frameworks.

To cite an interesting example, consider the so-called parapsychological phenomena, such as telepathy, clairvoyance, etc. A large number of self-proclaimed scientific thinkers advocate frameworks which reject parapsychological phenomena as fictional and non-existent. And there are a small number of thinkers who acknowledge parapsychological phenomena as genuine and authentic and investigate them. What is the difference between these two groups of thinkers? My answer: they operate with different categorial frameworks, one which rejects the category 'parapsychological' and the other which admits the category. According to the former, information about the world cannot be obtained without the instrumentality of our sensory channels and, insofar as alleged parapsychological phenomena violate this dictum, they are to be rejected as non-existent, fictional, and products of hoax and fraud; the latter, in contrast, allows for the possibility of acquiring information about the world without the operation of our sensory equipment. It is easy to see that in one framework all existence and phenomena are through and through physical, whereas in the other not all existence and phenomena are physical. This is the same as saying that one of the frameworks rejects the category 'disembodied mind' whereas the other admits it.

It should be obvious by now that the categorial framework a thinker is committed to and employs in his inquiry determines the areas of inquiry he acknowledges as rational, legitimate, and fruitful. This fact in itself clearly shows that we are fully justified in saying earlier that the kind of knowledge we produce depends not only on our physiological endowment but also on our psychological makeup, which includes the *emotional,* besides the mental. The commitment, which itself is not a matter wholly of intellect but of feeling and emotion, is what lies behind a thinker's acceptance or rejection of certain claims about the world. This is not to be construed as my saying that the choice of a categorial framework is arbitrary, irrational, and merely a matter of emotion; rather, what I am saying is that the choice is guided not only by what one construes to be rational, intellectual considerations but also by one's feelings and emotions, understood in the broadest sense of the terms. In a word, the knowledge we produce is a function of our physiological endowment, thought, and emotion. It is therefore a mistake to emphasize one of these to the exclusion of the others. We may now state as a central insight of *Jñāna-yoga* that the knowledge we produce is a function of our senses, intellect, and emotions; it is a grave error to think otherwise and emphasize one of these to the exclusion of the others.

I shall discuss two more examples in this context. Consider the framework underlying the Biblical account of man and other life-forms and that underlying Darwin's evolutionary account. The difference between the two, according to the upholders of the frameworks themselves, are far-reaching — as witness the vehement and interminable disputes and fierce legal battles and confrontations. One acknowledges the category of a creator-designer God and the other rejects it as irrelevant to a rational, scientific understanding of the panorama of life.

Let us consider magic, not magic based on sleight of hand but magic as real (as understood in certain archaic, modern, and contemporary circles). Almost all self-professed scientific frameworks reject magic in the second of the above senses as absurd and impossible, and belief in it as purely superstitious. What is the reason for this stance? Examine the frameworks and you will find out that one of them regards such magic as violating the principle of causation as well as that of conservation of matter-energy; whereas the other regards such magic as not only possible, in that it does not violate these principles, but actual. Thus what one regards as a rational possibility is itself determined by and reflected in one's own categorial framework.

I hope I have not been altogether unsuccessful in my attempts to enable the reader to attain a reasonably clear understanding of the concept of categorial framework in general. I have, as indicated earlier, deliberately refrained from presenting an example of a whole categorial framework in detail, along with a formal exhibition of its principles, rules, definitions, and categories.[1]

I shall bring this section to a close with a few pertinent observation concerning categorial frameworks. A system of logic is necessarily associated with every categorial framework. That is, a catalog of the principles of a categorial framework will include some logical principles. The study of a categorial framework consists of the study of not only each of its categories and principles but also of their interrelations. It is often the case that the proponent of a categorial framework also provides a justification of his framework. We shall say more later about such justifications. Sometimes one undertakes a comparative study of two or more frameworks, in order to bring out their relative merits, demerits, virtues, and limitations. Comparative study of this nature may be conducted among different frameworks in one and the same culture or among frameworks belonging to different cultures, one's own included. Thus one may, for example, compare Aristotle and Kant, Augustine and Aquinas, Kant and Śaṅkara, Aquinas and Rāmānuja, and so on.

I come now to a detailed consideration of the nature of categorial frameworks in general and of the knowledge they enable us to produce. In this discussion, I shall freely draw upon the works of two of the greatest *Jñāna-yogin*s — masters of the path of knowledge — namely, Śaṅkara,[2] the founder of *Advaita Vedānta* (with its foundations in the *Upaniṣad*s) and Nāgārjuna,[3] the great Buddhist philosopher and patriarch. I am not, however, concerned here with a systematic presentation and disquisition of their writings; rather, my aim is to present the essential insights of *Jñāna-yoga*, in light of my own study, reflection, and practice, all of which are inspired, aided, and facilitated by the teachings of these two sages.

The Principle of Superimposition: We have seen earlier that there are perfectly rational grounds to hold that beings constituted differently from each other necessarily make different sets of claims as to what the world is like. Thus sentient beings in other parts of the cosmos (leaving aside the question whether or not such beings in fact exist), insofar as they are constituted differently from us, experience the world and therefore describe it differently from the ways in which we, human beings, experience and describe the world. It is clear, then, that there is a reality which is experienced and described differently by differently constituted sentient beings in various parts of the cosmos. It is worth noting that even on this planet each type of sentient beings experiences the world differently — for example, the world of ants differs from that of, say, cats. It is an altogether different question whether cats and ants are capable of *describing* the world, 'describe' being understood in the sense in which human beings are said to describe the world. Whether or not certain types of sentient beings can describe the world, it is indisputable that different kinds of sentient beings *experience* the world differently. Thus a hungry tiger's experience of a deer (seeing a deer at a distance) is undoubtedly different from that of a hungry cow. It is to be further noted that experience and description of the world also vary from one culture to another; and, what is more, even in one and the same culture the experience and description of the world are different at different stages of its history. Thus, for instance, until not long ago the Ptolemaic system of astronomy and Biblical creationism dominated the Western intellectual tradition. That is, people in the Western world experienced and described the world according to Ptolemaic astronomy and the Bible. And it is well-known that at a later time these two modes of experience and description were replaced by Copernican astronomy and Darwinian biology.

What follows from the above considerations? There is a reality which is experienced and described differently by differently constituted beings. In order to clearly distinguish reality in this sense — as that which is experienced and described differently by differently constituted beings, as that which manifests itself differently to beings of different constitutions — from other senses of 'reality', we shall use the term 'ultimate reality' to refer to reality in the sense here specified. Thus there is an ultimate reality and it manifests itself·in different ways to differently constituted beings. How is it so? Because how ultimate reality manifests itself to beings of a certain kind depends upon the mode and manner of constitution of those beings. Each kind of beings, simply by virtue of their specific constitution, experience and describe the world in certain manners. Put differently, each type of beings experience and describe the world in a range of ways inextricably bound up with their constitution. Their constitution is the network, a glass if you will, through which beings of a certain kind experience and describe the world. The network is best understood as the total range of potentials for perception and conception of that kind of beings. One's experience and how one describes the experience are a function of one's powers of perception and conception, which are themselves founded in the psycho-physiological makeup of one's being. This observation leads us directly to the principle of superimposition: each kind of beings superimpose on ultimate reality percepts and concepts within the range of potentials for perception and conception allowed for by their constitution. In this manner, all expressible and communicable knowledge is at its foundation the product of the activity of superimposition (of percepts and concepts) on ultimate reality — what there is. It is of the highest importance to note that there can be no talk of the 'world' apart from superimposition. Percepts and concepts are called in Sanskrit *rūpa* (form) and *nāma* (name), respectively. 'Name' here is to be understood as concept, label, etc., not just in its ordinary sense as in: 'John' is my friend's name. It is through naming that thought organizes the content of experience — this is not an apple but a tennis ball.

It should immediately be clear that the principle of superimposition is not a contingent principle — a principle that could conceivably be false. Rather, it is a necessarily true principle, in that it is a statement of the foundations of the very possibility of experience and description — in a word, of knowledge itself. The principle itself is arrived at through *reflection* on our experience. It is a serious error to think that the principle is a product of experience or reason alone; on the contrary, it is unmistakably the result of reflection on our modes of being. This is to say that the distinction between experience and reason is not given in experience or reason itself. The distinction has its roots in reflection, which is not to be identified with experience or reason. If the reader thinks that the principle of superimposition can be refuted (falsified), let him inquire into the question: What does it mean to say that a sentient being experiences and describes the world in manners wholly dissociated from its own constitution? One will quickly see that it is impossible, in principle, for any type of sentient being to experience and describe the world in ways that have nothing to do with its psycho-physiological constitution.

The principle of superimposition is the most fundamental principle of *Jñāna-yoga*, for it clerly brings to our awareness the fact that all our experience and knowledge are bound up with the kind of beings we are. One might ask now: Is this not obvious? Where is the need to belabor something so obvious? My answer is: Yes, there is a sense in which the principle of superimposition is certainly obvious; but how many people are in fact aware of the principle? The point here is that the principle becomes obvious only on inquiry and reflection. And since most of us live unreflectively and uncritically, we are not aware of it. What is more, there are many, even among those who regard themselves as philosophers — in the sense of inquirers — who subscribe to the view (known as 'naive realism') that the world in itself is thus and such, independently of our psycho-physiological constitution. According to these people, the human being (or, for that matter, any sentient being) is merely a passive spectator and therefore his constitution has no bearing upon his experience and description of the world. This is to think, undoubtedly mistakenly, that the world in itself is of such characterizations as we attribute to it. If this is the case with regard to philosophers, one can easly imagine how far removed the ordinary person is from a knowledge and understanding of the principle of superimposition.

The principle of superimposition is well-known to such

Jñāna-yogins as Nāgārjuna and Śaṅkara. In fact, in the writings of Śaṅkara, superimposition is known as *adhyāsa*,[4] which may broadly be defined as follows: the activity on the part of the subject of attributing qualities, relations, etc. to something which it does not, in fact, possess. The attribution is always through some name (concept) and some form (percept). Thus each kind of sentient beings, under its own activity of superimposition, thinks that ultimate reality is thus and such. What each kind of sentient beings claims the world to be is inextricably bound up with its own range of potentials for perception and conception — in a word, with its own psycho-physiological constitution.

Superimposition, then, is the activity of imposing names and forms on the single reality which in itself is nameless and formless; for apart from superimposition there can be neither name nor form. It follows that superimposition is the only means by which expressible and communicable knowledge can be produced. All expressible knowledge, without exception, is thus the product of the activity of superimposition.

It is easy to see that a categorial framework is none other than a superimpositional framwork through which a given thinker attempts to grasp ultimate reality; in other words, a given inquirer's claims as to what the world is like necessarily stem from his superimpositional framework.

If we understand by the term 'world' the totality of various kinds of objects, events, poroperties, processes, relations, etc., then it is clear that without superimposition there can be no talk of the world. Thus the world is *not* ultimate reality but rather a description of ultimate reality as it manifests itself through some superimpositional framework or other. The question now arises: how many worlds are there? Answer: as many as the kinds of sentient beings in the cosmos. Thus the relation between ultimate reality and world is a one-many relation. This is simply to say that there is but a single (ultimate) reality and many worlds — the world of the so-called primitives, the mythic world, the everyday world, the scientific world (the world of science), the world of ants, the world of bees, the world of human

beings, the world of Andromedans (if there be such beings), and
so on, each world being the product of the psycho-physiological
constitution of a certain kind of beings. This same point may be
made somewhat differently: thinkers from different parts of the
cosmos all agree that there is a reality; but they disagree as to
what the reality is like. This means that the disagreement is not
about whether there is a reality but rather about the various
descriptions of that reality as grasped and formulated through
different name-form networks — superimpositional, categorial
frameworks. It is noteworthy that even among beings constituted
alike, say human beings, there are bound to be disagreements
among their descriptions of reality, the disagreements being due
to differences in the conceptual components of their
superimpositional frameworks. This is to say that it is possible
for there to be perceptual agreement along with conceptual
disagreement. Thus, to take an example, according to Aristotle,
objects like stones fall to the ground when released because all
things seek their natural places, and since the Earth is the
natural place of stones they fall to the ground. However,
according to Newton, stones fall to the ground because of the
gravitational force exerted by the Earth on them. It is to be
understood that Aristotle and Newton agree — perceptual
agreement — that stones released fall to the ground; they
disagree as to why they do so — conceptual disagreement.
Similarly, for the so-called primitives, trees, rivers, and
mountains are spirits, whereas for modern man they are just
trees, rivers, and mountains and any talk of their being spitits
is simply absurd and superstitious. This once again illustrates
conceptual disagreement along with perceptual agreement.
One might object to this observation by saying that the primitives
also *perceive* trees, rivers, and mountains as spirits, not just so
conceive of them. The objection is that the primitives' conception
makes a difference to the way they perceive these objects. My
answer to this objection is that there is no need to deny that such
is indeed the case; it should, however, be emphasized that there
is a perceptual agreement (overlap) between the primitives and
modern man, to the extent that they both label the *same* objects
as trees, rivers, and mountains; the disagreement between

them may be characterized as follows: the primitives also perceive them as spirits, whereas modern man does not so perceive them. Why is this so? Because the primitive's perceiving these objects as also spirits is a consequence of his superimpositional framework, and modern man's not perceiving them as spirits is a result of the conceptual component of his categorial framework. The point, then, is that while we grant perceptual differences between the primitive and modern man, we trace those differences to differences in the conceptual elements of their respective superimpositional frameworks. As such, the above objection does not militate against but is in full harmony with our central thesis that all expressible and communicable knowledge is the product of the activity of superimposition. Thus, interestingly enough, the objection, when clarified and answered, adds strength to the principle of superimposition by leading to the observation that what — a description — one claims to perceive is itself determined by one's categorial framework. That there is something — the source of sensory stimuli — is the perceptual; what that something is, is the conceptual. That which presents itself to us, the perceptual component (of knowledge) is categorized and organized by the conceptual component. Put differently, evey knowledge-claim has a form and a content; the former is grounded in conceptual activity and the latter in perception. Let it be noted that 'perception' here is to be understood in the broad sense as including what we call 'external perception' (seeing a tree in the yard) and 'internal perception' (a mental image, a feeling of pain, etc.). Thus in the case of logico-mathematical knowledge-claims, their content pertains to internal perception. Someone might object to this observation by saying that logico-mathematical knowledge-claims are devoid of any content. The answer to this objection is that if these claims have no content at all, how and in what manner can one account for the undeniable and central fact of logico-mathematical activity as one of creating and assigning forms and generating from them other forms, from which still other forms, and so on? The point is that where there is no content there can be no possibility of plurality of forms, either. The content of logico-mathematical knowledge-claims is one of *meanings* and it is meanings that are internally perceived. Different meanings are represented by different forms, and in this manner arise different forms and systems of forms, such as arithmetic, algebra, geometry, set theory, and so on. Thus, for instance, if one does not distinguish between the meanings 'square' and 'square-root', one cannot represent them by different forms, except purely vacuously. It is to be noted that a given meaning-content can be expressed in more than one form by performing operations according to the definitions, axioms, and rules of inference of the system (to which the forms belong); thus, to give an example, 1/2 and 0.5 are two different forms for the same meaning; similarly, $(x + y)$ $(x - y)$ and $(x^2 - y^2)$ are two different forms for the same meaning-content. It should be clear by now that meanings are not objects of external percetion but rather of internal perception. In light of these considerations, 'perception' in the context of superimposition is to be understood as including both external and internal perceptions. It is important to note that every knowledge-claim has both a form and a content, although the content of some knowledge-claims, such as in logic and mathematics, can only be perceived internally.

I come now to an examination of the question of truth and falsity of knowledge-claims. From what has been said earlier, it is clear that every knowledge-claim arises in and is bound up with, implicitly or explicitly, with some categorial — superimpositional — framework or other. There simply cannot be a knowledge-claim apart from some categorial framework. Accordingly, in order to understand a knowledge-claim and certify its truth or falsity, one needs to familiarize oneself with the categorial framework on which the knowledge-claim is based. Without such familiarity, one will not be able to comprehend the knowledge-claim and may even dismiss it as meaningless and absurd. Let me illustrate all this. Consider the knowledge-claim that electrons are negatively charged particles. This knowledge-claim arises from (belongs to) the categorial framework underlying modern physics, and only those conversant with this framework will be able to understand the knowledge-claim and also know how to determine its truth or falsity. That is, the various procedures and criteria by which one is to determine the truth or falsity of the claim are bound up with the categorial framework. And if the knowledge-claim that electrons are negatively charged particles is presented to someone — say, an inhabitant of the Amazon jungle — who is totally ignorant of the underlying categorial framework, it will be wholly incomprehensible to him; and one can easily imagine him exclaiming, "you people are really strange and say things even stranger and downright meaningless and bizarre." Does this mean, then, that the above knowledge-claim is true only to us, members of modern scientific communities, and absurd and false to the Amazonian Indian? Certainly not, for, this is an important point, the Amazonian Indian can learn our categorial framework and how to operate with it, including the methods and procedures by which to produce knowledge-claims and determine their truth or falsity. Simply bring an Amazonian Indian baby, raise him in the U.S., put him through our shcools and univeristies, and he will say, "yes, there are such entities as electrons and they are negatively charged particles." What this shows is that the ability to learn and operate with our categorial framework is within the range of potentials for perception and conception of the Aamazonian Indian. And this should not be surprising, for the Amazonian Indian is a member of our species, and to say that he is a member of our species is to say that he is constituted as we are; and to be constituted as we are is to be endowed with the same range of potentials for perception and conception as we are. All this is possible because of the simple fact that being members of the same species all of us are constituted alike, and *vice versa*.

The above considerations, along with the illustration, lead to the following conclusion: Every expressible and communicable knowledge-claim, insofar as it arises in and is bound up with some superimpositional framework, comes to have meaning and truth (as well as falsity) in light of that framework. The knowledge-claim has neither meaning nor truth nor falsity outside of the framework. Thus the claim that there are entities called 'protons' and that they are positively charged particles is meaningful to and certifiable by any inquirer who understands and operates with the framework which underlies modern physics. It goes without saying that certain knowledge-claims of the Amazonian Indian, which at first strike us as meaningless and superstitious, will become meaningful to and certifiable by us on our learning his categorial framework. That we can learn and operate with the Amazonian Indian's framework should be no more surprising than that he can learn and operate with ours, since he and we, being members of the same species, are similarly constituted. As long as each is ignorant of the other's framework, each finds the other's knowledge-claims puzzling and absurd; for is it not true that the Amazonian Indian's talk of gods and spirits sounds at first to us as superstitious nonsense, as our talk of electromagnetic waves, quasars, the double helix, etc. does to him? From the standpoint of our own categorial framework, we regard him and his claims as ignorant and superstitious, just as he does ours from the standpoint of his own framework. It is only when each set of knowledge-claims is seen and grasped from within its own categorial framework that it becomes meaningful and certifiable as true or false. This brings us to the topic of the relativity of all knowledge-claims, which I shall now consider.

We have shown that no knowledge-claim can have meaning and truth (or falsity) apart from some superimpositional framework or other which gives rise to it. This is the same as saying that the meaning and truth (or falsity) of a given knowledge-claim is always relative to — in reference to — some categorial framework. Thus, for example, the claim, "positrons are positively charged particles", taken in isolation, that is, dissocated from a categorial framework, has neither meaning nor truth nor falsity. It is only when viewed from the categorial framework in which it is generated that the claim acquires meaning and truth. In other words, the knowledge-claim that positrons are positively charged particles is a *relative* truth. This same observation holds with regard to knowledge-claims emanating from different superimpositional frameworks. To take another example, the claim that DNA has the structure of double helix is meaningful and true only within the categorial framework underlying modern biology, in particular molecular genetics. Take the claim out of that framework, it ceases to have either meaning or truth. It is of the highest importance to note that apart from the framework the claim cannot even be formulated. Thus it is the supermipositional framework itself that makes possible — brings into being, if you will — a given knowledge-claim. It is therefore quite correct to say that every knowledge-claim, insofar as it is expressible and communicable, is meaningful and true (or false) only relative to some categorial framework or other. This same point may be made by saying that categorical frameworks can only produce relative truths. Thus all branches of knowledge, such as physics, chemistry, economics, physiology, philosophy, etc., are systems of relative truths — truths inalienably bound up with categorial frameworks. Every knowledge-claim, irrespective of its subject-matter and no matter how well-established, is *necessarily* a relative truth, insofar as it is generated and validated within some categorial framework. It is thus an irrefutable truth that such is the nature of categorial knowledge, knowledge producible through categorial frameworks. Someone might now ask: "are you saying that all our rational-scientific inquiries only give us relative truths?" The answer is unequivocally in the affirmative: yes, they can only enable us to produce relative truths. But, I wish to ask, why do many people find this conclusion disturbing and dissatisfying? Why is one provoked to express shock, dismay, and profound discontent at the announcement that categorial frameworks enable us, in principle, to produce only relative truths? It will be instructive and revealing to answer these questions.

Let it be noted at the outset that human beings in all ages have felt gnawing discomfort, nagging disquietude, and deadening discontent with the notion of relative truth — as witness the contempt and derogation lavishly heaped upon those who teach the relativity of all categorial knowledge. Many have called, in an accusing and belittling tone of voice, 'relativists' the teachers of the relativity of categorial knowledge. Once identified as the purveyors of relativity, it is but a short step to look down upon the teachers of relativity as dishonest, immoral, corrupt, and dangerous human beings. In short, the idea of relativity has acquired for itself scathing notoriety and palpable disrespect in the eyes of its opponents — majority of mankind. What is the reason for this state of affairs? The reason, I submit, is to be sought in a chronic and crippling misunderstanding as to the whole notion of relative truth. The misunderstanding consists of instinctively and uncritically identifying relative truth with falsehood. Thus, for instance, as soon as people hear someone declare that the claim that the Earth goes around the Sun is a *relative* truth, their immediate reaction is to construe the speaker as having proclaimed a falsehood. And if these people were asked as to what is objectionable to the view that the claim is a relative truth, they would say that it has been established by science to be an unquestionable, absolute truth. Laboring under short-lived memory, these people forget that not long ago the reigning scientific claim was that the Sun moved around a stationary Earth. What escapes these people is the question that if some claim is an absolute truth, how could it at a later time be rejected as false and replaced by another? For, after all, absolute truth is truth that cannot by its very nature be questioned, rejected, and replaced. To take another example, prior to the advent of modern biology and geology, it was regarded as an absolute truth by many in the Western world that the Earth is only six-thousand years old, and any suggestion that the Earth is far older is rejected as false and heretical. But we all know that in our own day the claim that the Earth is about five-billion years old is accepted as an absolute truth, firmly established by science. How is one to account for this strange and bewildering phenomenon?

The main point here is that many people, in their unquenchable thirst for absolute truths, unconsciously and unthinkingly identify relative truth with falsehood; for nothing less than absolute truth satisfies them. But, strangely enough, seldom have these people bothered to undertake a critical examination of the concepts of absolute truth and relative truth and inquired into the ways in which they are to be produced and certified. They are, as a rule, wholly oblivious to the activity of superimposition on the part of the inquirer and hence to the concept of categorial framework. These people are sure of one thing: absolute truths are the only truths worth possessing, and anything other than absolute truth is plain falsehood, unworthy of the effort and attention of true inquirers.

But is one justified in regarding relative truth as falsehood? The answer is definitely in the negative: no, to say that a given claim is a relative truth is *not* to say that it is false; rather, it is to say that the claim will be certified as true by all inquirers who are constituted alike and who conduct their inquiry according to the superimpositional framework within which in the first place the claim arises and is determined to be true. Recall our example with the Amazonian Indian and you will see the point. The knowledge-claim that electrons are negaitvely charged particles is a relative truth, in the sense that it has meaning and truth not in isolation but only relative to a certain categorial framework. The Amazonian Indian, ignorant of this framework, first dismisses the claim as meaningless and incomprehensible. But on learning the categorial framework and operating with it, he certifies the claim to be true. It is clear, then, that 'relative truth' does not mean falsehood; rather, it means truth emanating from and certifiable within a specific superimpositional framework. Only those who are blinded by their passion for absolute truth will mistakenly think that relative truth is nothing short of falsehood. Let it be noted further that understanding relative truth as truth bound up with a given categorial framework is in full conformity with the spirit of rational-scientific inquity. For the history of rational-scientific inquiry is replete with instances where something regarded as immutable truth today will be considered false tomorrow, and something counted as false yesterday will be proclaimed as unblemished truth today. It should be abundantly clear from these observations that there can be no room for absolute and final truths in any rational-scientific enterprise; for as an inquirer shifts from one categorial framework to another, the truth and falsehood of knowledge-claims also change. In a word, all rational-scientific truths are tentative, subject to revision and modification, and even outright rejection at a later time.

A categorial framework, by its very nature, is a delimiting mechanism. By this I mean that every categorial framework includes within itself and regards as legitimate certain perceptual-conceptual possibilities and excludes others (from among the perceptual-conceptual possibilities defining the range of potentials for perception and conception of beings of a certain constitution). As a result, when an inquirer switches from one categorial framework to another, he will find that, in light of the new categorial framework, knowledge-claims hitherto certified as true are no longer true and those previously considered as false are no longer false. It is in this manner that rational-scientific inquiries are conducted with ever-changing superimpositional frameworks. The need to move from one framework to another may arise from a shift in the perceptual component, the conceptual component, or both.[5]

Since it is in the very nature of a categorial framework to include within itself certain perceptual-conceptual possibilities and exclude others, it follows that there can be no such thing as an all-inclusive categorial framework. In fact, the concept of an all-inclusive framework is self-contridictory and vacuous. It is self-contradictory because a categorial framework cannot crystallize itself and come into being unless it excludes certain perceptual-conceptual possibilities; it is vacuous in the sense that if someone were to propose a certain categorial framework as an all-inclusive one, it will be totally useless in the production of knowledge-claims. The reason for this is that what makes a categorial framework productive of knowledge-claims is the *tension* between the included and the excluded perceptual-conceptual possibilities; and since such tension is wholly absent in the case of an all-inclusive framework, it is devoid of any power to produce knowledge-claims. To illustrate this point analogically, it will be impossible to construct a thermodynamic engine, which operating in cycles, will convert thermal energy into work if all bodies in the universe are at the same temperature, whatever it may be; that is, just as a temperature-difference is necessary for the possibility of a thermodynamic engine, so also the tension between the included and the excluded is necessary for the possibility of a categorial framework. Or, to take another example, a stone attached to one end of a string will be maintained in a circular path by whirling the string by holding it in hand at the other end. What keeps the stone in the circular orbit? Answer: the tension in the string. Cut the string, loosen the grip, or simply stop whirling, the stone will no longer be on the circle. Reason? The tension necessary to maintain the stone in its circular path is absent, and this results in the collapse of the system.

It should unmistakably be clear from the foregoing that the knowledge-claims generated by *any* categorial framework are necessarily relative truths (or relative falsehoods), 'relative' being understood as relative to that framework. There simply cannot be any expressible and communicable knowledge-claims which are not associated with (relative to) some categorial framework or other. There is nothing wrong with relative truths, and to lament that categorial frameworks can only produce relative truths is like grumbling that one has only air to breathe and food to eat. Just as no elixir of immortality can be found in a milieu of ever-changing world, so also no absolute truths can be found in a milieu of ever-changing superimpositional frameworks. To look for absolute truths in categorial knowledge — knowledge producible through the instrumentality of categorial frameworks — is to betray fundamental ignorance as to the nature and function of categorial frameworks. Only those who are incurably possessed of a penchant for absolute truths and who have not in the first place inquired into the concept of absolute truth look for absolute truths in categorial knowledge. This brings us to a consideration of the distinction between absolute truth and universal truth.

Many people, philosophers or otherwise, uncritically (I say 'uncritically', as will become clear in the sequel), think and teach that universal truth and absolute truth are one and the same. A mere glance at any philosophic work by Western thinkers in general will show that they indeed mean and use the terms 'universal truth' and 'absolute truth' synonymously. But they have not arrived at this identification through any inquiry; rather, they only have a strong feeling that universal truth and absolute truth cannot but be the same. Such a feeling itself is based on some vague considerations as the following: 'Absolute truth' means truth, the same, to everyone, every being, every inquirer, irrespective of their manners of constitution and modes of being; and 'universal truth' means truth, the same, in every nook and corner of the universe — for example, the law of gravitation. No one can deny it. Why? Because it is true for everyone, everywhere, and everywhen, as it were, across the universe. Thus universal truth and absolute truth are one and the same. We shall now show that, according to *Jñāna-yoga*, such a view is mistaken.

We have established earlier that every expressible and communicable knowledge-claim is necessarily tied up with some categorial framework or other, and that every knowledge-claim generatable within a framework is a relative truth (or falsehood) — that is, relative to the framework. This is the same as saying that there can be no expressible and communicable truth apart from some categorial framework. If so, how and in what manner do the concepts of universal truth and absolute truth arise in the first place? He who thinks that universal truth (the same, according to him, as absolute truth) is truth, the same, for everyone, everywhere, and everywhen, regardless of any and all conditions and circumstances whatever, should ask himself, "how can there be any truth, relative or absolute (universal), independently of everyone and everything? What precisely do I mean by 'absolute truth' and how do I come to know it? If there be an absolute truth, can one, in principle, articulate it?" According to *Jñāna-yoga*, he who claims absolute truth expressible and communicable is wholly ablivious to the fundamental fact of the activity of superimposition on the part of the inquirer and therewith to the instrumentality of superimpositional frameworks in the production of knowledge-claims, that is, to the perceptual-conceptual networks which each thinker of a certain type of constitution brings with himself as an integral part of his mode of being; he is further ignorant of the fact that therefore every knoledge-claim as well as its truth (or falsity) is inseparably bound up with the superimpositional framework. It is precisely because of this ignorance that he fails to see that all truths producible through categorial frameworks are relative truths and goes on to claim that the truths produced by his own framework as absolute (universal) truths. But, one might ask now, what axactly is the diference between universal truth and absolute truth? The answer to this question is based on one of the profound insights of *Jñāna-yoga* and is as follows.

Universal truth and absolute truth are *not* the same. Universal truth is truth that is certifiable as such by all inquirers constituted alike and who operate with a certain categorial framework. This is to say that universal truth is truth that is species-bound. Insofar as any truth is expressible and communicable, it is necessarily species-bound. It is the aim and goal of the various departments of knowledge, such as mathematics, physics, chemistry, biology, psychology, etc., to produce universal truths in their respective domains of inquiry. Thus when an American physicist announces certain knowledge-claims as resulting from his studies, another physicist, for example, from Japan, will be able to scrutinize the knowledge-claims by conducting theoretical and experimental investigations and thereby declare whether the knowledge-claims of the American physicist are true or false. The Japanese physicist cannot even understand, let alone confirm or disconfirm, the knowledge-claims of the American physicist except from the standpoint of the latter's categorial framework underlying those claims. Stated explicitly, the American and Japanese physicists, both being members of the same species — similarly constituted — and operating with the same categorial framework, the one upholding modern physics, are able to understand each other's knowledge-claims and certify them to be true or false. Is it not absurd, then, to think that every inquirer in the universe, regardless of his makeup and framework, will also validate our physicists' knowledge-claims? Universal truths are ineluctably species-bound; and insofar as inquirers in other parts of the universe are constituted differently from us, human beings, they experience and describe the world and go about it differently than we do. Universal truths, then, are first and foremost relative truths; and relative truths, on being validated by an ever-increasing number of inquirers inhabiting different parts of the same spatio-temporal segment of the cosmos, acquire stability and wide currency, thereby attaining to the title of 'universal truths', 'laws of Nature', and so on.

Absolute truths are truths independent of the psycho-physiological constitution of any and all inquirers and cannot therefore be expressed and communicated. And if someone advances a knowledge-claim as an absolute truth, it can easily be shown to be bound up with some superimpositional framework, often his own; this in turn means that the advanced knowledge-claim is not an absolute truth but rather a relative truth. It follows from these considerations that the locution "expressible and communicable absolute truth" is a contradiction in terms; for no categorial framework can ever give rise to an absolute truth. We therefore conclude that universal truth and absolute truth are not the same but quite different. We shall later discuss the question whether or not there is absolute truth, although inexpressible and incommunicable.

It will be instructive to examine why people lay absolute claims on behalf of truths generated from within their own categorial frameworks. The explanation of this ageold and pervasive myopia constitutes yet another insight of *Jñāna-yoga*.

Confronting the world as something other than himself, man embarks on the search for the knowledge of the world as non-self (the other). But knowledge is always a relation between the knower and the known in that it brings the two together. That is, knowledge is the means by which man seeks to unite the self and the other. In this manner, the thirst for knowledge is at bottom the quest for being. Put differently, in his very attempt to know the world man appropriates the world to himself. But what is knowledge and how is it produced? We have already seen that knowledge, insofar as it is expressible and communicable at all, is made up of propositions, which in turn are constituted of concepts (names) and percepts (forms). Accordingly, the reality which one creates through one's knowledge is the reality of names and forms, and not reality as it is in itself. But in their thirst for the absolute and the unconditioned, people forget this and mistake the reality they construct out of names and forms for reality itself. Thus they are like thirsty travelers in a desert who, not knowing the difference between reality and illusion, are tempted by the mirage and rush in vain from place to place hoping to quench their thirst. But just as mirages cannot quench our thirst, so also imaginative constructions of reality — products of superimpositional frameworks — cannot quench man's thirst for the absolute, the unconditioned, and the ultimate. Man thus becomes a wanderer in the jungle of his own imaginative constructions of realality. The failure to distinguish between reality in itself and the reality of names and forms is ignorance (*avidyā*), which inevitably breeds pain and suffering. Each school of thought, in its thirst for the absolute and quest for being, claims absolute truth and validity for its own knowledge-claims — theories, views, doctrines — and condemns those of others as false and misguided. Consequently, views of reality — philosophies — become dogmatic, and dogmatism produces blindness, conflict, opposition, and intolerance. In sum, then, it is the thirst for the knowledge of the absolute and the unconditioned, which at heart is none other than the quest for being, that makes people ignorantly lay absolute claims on behalf of truths produced from within their own categorial frameworks.

If someone doubts that the thirst for the knowledge of the absolute is at once the quest for being, let him, at his earliest opportunity, make critical and disparaging remarks, in the presence of an adherent, about some system of thought, be it Platonism, Aristotelianism, Kantianism, Capitalism, Marxism, Biblical creationism, Darwinism, Freudianism, Behaviorism, and so on. He will immediately discover that the adherents will react to his remarks as if they were personally attacked. What is the reason for such a reaction? Every thinker unconsciously identifies himself with the categorial framework he subscribes to, and because of this identification he deems any attack on the framework (and the associated knowledge-claims) as an attack on himself. But, one might wonder, what is the reason for one's identifying oneself with one's own categorial framework? Answer: because his thirst for knowledge is at once his quest for being. This is to say that one's categorial framework is not just an instrument of knowledge but is one's very being — one has extraordinary, life-and-death stakes in one's framework. One's being is clear and secure as long as one's categorial framework is not under attack. For this reason, any assault on the framework becomes a source of menacing anxiety, and hence every attack has to be staved off. In brief, the invulnerability of one's categorial framework is the invulnerability of one's own being. Thus ideological conflicts, irrespective of the field in which they might occur, whether in philosophy, politics, economics, science, etc., are really conflicts between persons or groups of persons who have identified themselves with conflicting frameworks and associated world-views. And we all know only too well the pain and suffering that result from ideological conflicts. Let it be emphasized that ideologies in themselves do not have the power to make wars in any form, physical, psychological, intellectual, etc., but only people possessed of ideologies, people who have identified themselves with ideologies, which always arise from and sustain themselves through categorial frameworks. Do we not often hear someone praised and lauded as a passionate defender of a certain standpoint (a categorial framework and the knowledge-claims flowing from it)? But why passionate defence? Because, for all intents and purposes, the standpoint is the defender himself.

Our discussion of relative truth, universal truth, and absolute truth naturally leads us to a consideration of objectivity and objective truth (objective knowledge), to which I shall now turn. One might ask: "If there can be no expressible and communicable truths apart from some categorial framework and hence the truths producible through categorial frameworks can only be relative truths, are we not, then, to eschew the notions of objectivity and objective truth, thereby casting grave doubts on rational-scientific enterprises, long regarded as paradigmatic of objective truths and objectivity itself?" According to the popular and dominant view, both within and without the academia, objective truth is truth which has nothing whatsoever to do with any and all inquirers. In other words, objective truth is truth independent of inquirers. It should be apparent from our discussion of the principle of superimposition and categorial frameworks that there can, in principle, be no such thing as objective truth as understood in the above sense — independent of inquirers. Such a concept of objective truth is self-contradictory and can only be a figment of imagination nurtured by ignorance and dogmatism. According to *Jñāna-yoga*, objective truth is none other than universal truth, not absolute truth as is mistakenly believed by many. Universal truth, we have seen, is truth certifiable by all inquirers of a certain kind of makeup operating with a given framework. Thus, for example, the knowledge-claim that the structure of DNA is a double helix is a universal truth; and it is objectively true, in the sense that all biologists who are of the same psycho-physiological constitution as that of human beings and who conduct their inquiry according to the categorial framework underlying the above knowledge-claim will certify it to be true. In a word, it is an objective truth. 'Objective truth' does not mean truth independent if inquirers; rather, it means truth determinable by all inquirers of a certain constitution by not allowing their idiosyncrasies — prejudices, whims, and fancies — to affect the categorial framework in which the knowledge-claim arises in the first place and in light of which it is also to be tested. What *else* could one possibly ask for in the name of objective truth? None. Thus it is best to dispense altogether with the concept of objective truth, with its absurd and misleading connotation, and use instead the concept of intersubjective truth. But so long as one understands by 'objective truth' no more and no less than intersubjective truth, no harm is done in continuing to use the term 'objective truth'.

Objectivity, then, is nothing but intersubjectivity. Something is an objective truth only insofar as it is certifiable as true by differe *subjects* (inquirers). Objectivity is simply the capacity on the part of investigators to set aside their own prejudices and predilections from distorting the framework from withing which they produce knowledge-claims and determine their truth. It is worth noting that there could be no talk of objectivity and objective truth if there were exactly one inquirer in the universe. Think of a sole and single occupant of the universe proclaiming, "I am now going to construct an objective system of knowledge of the world." Objectivity and objective truth thus presuppose a *plurality* of inquirers of a certain kind of constitution. To conclude, objectivity is intersubjectivity and objective truth intersubjective truth. Objective truths are universal, species-bound truths, which are but relative truths validatable by a plurality of inquirers of similar makeup, all conducting their investigation according to a given superimpositional framework.

In light of the foregoing analyses, there are no grounds at all to think that the fact that categorial frameworks can only enable us to produce relative truths vitiates rational-scientific endeavors, and therewith objectivity and objective knowledge and truth. If anything, one only comes to a clearer understanding and deeper appreciation of the fact that categorial frameworks are at the heart of all rational-scientific investigations. We also become keenly aware that all knowledge and truth have their source in the inquirer and unmistakably bear his stamp. For is it not strange and absurd to think that the knowledge and truths we produce should be wholly dissociated from the kind of beings we are? Further, why should we think that for our knowledge and truth to be truly objective beings constitutionally different from us should also certify them? Have we not produced objective, rational-scientific knowledge without concerning ourselves with beings inhabiting other parts of the cosmos? How other kinds of beings are constituted and how they experience and describe the world has no bearing whatever on the objectivity of our systems of knowledge and truth. Is our physics any the less true, objective, and efficacious because we have not yet had it validated by Andromedans? Let us therefore not worry about how other kinds of beings know the world and do their physics. It is enough and salutary to be aware that what kind of physics they produce, if at all, depends on their constitution and their superimpositional frameworks — in a word, on their modes of being.

We shall now take up the question as to why and how one categorial framework comes to be displaced and replaced by another. We have shown earlier that there can, in principle, be no such thing as "an all-encompassing categorial framework", since the very concept of such a framework is a contradiction in terms. What this remarkable insight of *Jñāna-yoga* means, then, is that no categorial framework is capable of exhaustively dealing with the multifarious facets of our experience. Every categorial framework is a delimiting instrument, in that it necessarily excludes from itself certain perceptions and conceptions among the range of our potentials for perception and conception. And since without such an exclusion no categorial framework can even come into being, it is quite correct to say, paradoxical as it may sound, that every categorial framework depends, in a fundamental sense, as much on the excluded as on the included. We have hitherto pointed out that the tension between the included and the excluded sustains the framework. Remove the tension by total inclusion or total exclusion, and there can be no categorial framework. Total inclusion means an all-encompassing framework, which, in principle, is impossible; on the other hand, total exclusion means there is no need for a framework at all. Thus in either case there can be no categorial framework. The essential point here, then, is that every categorial framework leads to situations in which it breaks down. It is of the highest importance to note that the breakdown of a categorial framework is testimony to the tension between the included and the excluded. That is, it is none other than inquiry into the included, through the instrumentality of a given categorial framework, that leads — nay, compels — the inquirer to a consideration of the excluded. The tension between the included and the excluded thus at once sustains the framework and brings about its breakdown and replacement. Why does one want to replace a given framework which has served one so long and well? Answer: inquiry from within the framework itself gives rise to questions and problems which, paradoxically enough, could not be satisfactorily answered and solved by the percepts, concepts, definitions, rules, methods, procedures, and criteria dictated by the framework itself. It is in this manner that every categorial framework points beyond itself to what is excluded. Examples of replacement of superimpositional frameworks abound in man's intellectual history.[6] Some of the best known are the following: Ptolemaic (geocentric) astronomy by Copernican (heliocentric) astronomy, Aristotelian physics by Galilean-Newtonian physics, Newtonian physics by Einsteinian physics, classical physics by quantum physics, Biblical creationism by Darwinian biology and modern geology, scholasticism by modern philosophy, and so on. The periodic but inevitable replacement of one categorial framework by another clearly points to the relativity of all categorial knowledge-claims and truths generatable from within a categorial framework. For if geocentric astronomy were absolutely true, how could it be displaced and replaced, as it actually was, by heliocentric astronomy? Is it not true that Alexander Pope sang and mused rhapsodically about the *immutable* truths of Newtonian physics? And is it not the case that even today many regard heliocentric astronomy as an absolutely true description of our solar system? But none of this should be surprising if we remember that people, in their thirst for knowledge of the absolute which is none other than the quest for being, attach themselves to and identify with frameworks. In any case, it should by now be amply clear that every categorial framework, simply by virtue of being a framework, sooner or later leads to its own breakdown and replacement. It is none other than this fact that is reflected in the characterization of rational-scientific (categorial) truths as not finalities and absolute truths but rather tentative and relative. That our experience of the world is such that no categorial framework can ever capture it in its variety, multiplicity, and totality and that man has been constantly constructing categorial frameworks under which to subsume ever larger sets of phenomena are an eloquent tribute at once to the creativity of the world and of the human spirit. There are thus no grounds to lament that an all-encompassing categorial framework is for ever unavailable and that categorial frameworks can only enable us to produce relative knowledge-claims and relative truths, but never absolute ones. On the contrary, clear understanding and recognition of this fact are cause for joyous celebration of man and the world as the very source of creativity.

Those who command the above insight of *Jñāna-yoga* into the nature of expressible and communicable knowledge do not attach themselves to and identify themselves with any categorial frameworks, and refrain from making absolute claims on behalf of any categorial truth. Only the ignorant and the deluded lay dogmatic and absolute claims for their own categorial truths.

But, one might wonder, what exactly happens when a categorial truth — relative truth — is claimed to be absolute? This question is analyzed in great detail in one of the most profound works of *Jñāna-yoga*: the *Mūla-madhyamaka-kārikā*,[7] by Nāgārjuna (AD 1-2), the great Buddhist sage, philosopher, and patriarch. Nāgārjuna's technique of analysis is known as *prasaṅga* (usually translated as 'dialectic'), which may be described as follows. The technique is employed to demonstrate the untenability of any categorial truth *advanced as absolute truth*, by showing that such a claim is self-contradictory — engenders a contradiction — and therefore false. Thus Nāgārjuna takes a thesis (a view) as stated by its proponent and, by employing the definitions, propositions, principles, rules, and procedures of the advocate's own categorial framework, proceeds to demonstrate that the thesis at hand, insofar as it is claimed to be absolute, is self-contradictory; and since the proponent of the thesis himself acknolwdges freedom from contradiction as necessary condition for its truth, he has now to withdraw his claim of absolute truth on behalf of the thesis. It is clear, then, that the upholder of the thesis could himself have discovered the self-contradictory nature of his thesis, claimed as absolute, were it not for the fact that in his thirst for the absolute and the unconditioned he was held captive by his own imaginative construction of reality and fell victim to illusion and dogmatism.

Nāgārjuna's method of *prasaṅga* is often referred to as *reductio ad absurdum* (reducing to absurdity). But it is important to bear in mind that there is a fundamental difference between the *reductio ad absurdum* of Nāgārjuna and the commonly known one of the Western tradition. Thus, for Nāgārjuna, unlike in the Western tradition, the demonstration of the falsity of a thesis does *not* entail the truth of its antithesis. Let us schematically illustrate this point. Let T be the thesis claimed by a thinker to be absolutely true. Nāgārjuna analyzes T in light of the categorial framework in which it arose and shows that T implies a proposition, say P, as well as its negation, not-P, and concludes T to be false, with the clear warning that the falsity of T does not mean the truth of its antithesis, namely, not-T. The underlying insight here is that in its own turn not-T can be shown to be self-contradictory and hence false. In contrast, in the Western version, a thinker starts out with the aim of establishing the truth of T. He assumes that T is false and obtains from this assumption a proposition, say Q, and its negation, namely, not-Q; he then concludes that T is true, insofar as the assumption of its falsity leads to a contradiction. Thus, for instance, Zeno of Elea, having shown by *reductio ad absurdum,* that the Heraclitean thesis — reality is of the nature of pure flex (change) — is self-contradictory, goes on to claim that therefore its antithesis — the Parmenidean claim that reality is One, unchanging, and eternal — is true. According to Nāgārjuna, Zeno is not entitled to such a move because the Parmenidean thesis too can be shown to be self-contradictory and false, insofar as it is advanced as an absolute truth. This is to say that every categorial thesis for which absolute claims are laid is self-contradictory and therefore false. It is precisely for this reason that neither Nāgārjuna nor any other *Jñāna-yogin* attaches himself to any thesis about the unconditioned and the ultimate.

I shall now illustrate the method of *prasaṅga* by presenting Nāgārjuna's analysis of the concept of causality (causation). Let it be immediately noted that Nāgārjuna has no objection to the notion of cause as that which produces effect(s) and to the employment of the concept of causality as part and parcel of a categorial framework in the investigation of phenomena in order to arrive at knowledge-claims. Rather, what is at issue is the nature of the relation between cause and effect — whether cause and effect are identical (effect pre-exists in the cause) or different (effect does not pre-exist in the cause). It is to be noted that some inquirers developed frameworks in which cause and effect are *absolutely* identical and others those in which cause and effect are *absolutely* different. Nāgārjuna proposes to examine four logically possible alternative views concerning cause and effect:

1.   a thing arises out of itself

2.   a thing arises out of a not-self;

3.   a thing arises out of both itself and a not-self;

4.   a thing arises neither out of itself nor out of a not-self.

Consider thesis 1. If effect and cause are identical, in the sense that the former pre-exists in the latter, then there can be no difference between the two, and it simply does not make sense to talk about causality; for causality is a relation between two things, and for it to be a genuine relation there must be a difference between the cause and its effect. But if one identifies cause and its effect, one renders the whole concept of causality meaningless. Furthermore, it would not do either to argue that cause and effect are identical in some respects and different in others. For if the cause and effect are indentical in just those respects that are relevant to causation, then the claim that cause and effect are different in other respects is irrelevant, and causation is still unexplained. On the other hand, if cause and effect are different in just those respects that are relevant to causation, then surely the thesis that cause and effect are identical is manifestly false. Thus in either case the claim that cause and effect are identical is absurd. All this can be expressed by saying that if cause and effect are identical, then everything that can be affirmed or denied of the one should also be capable of being affirmed or denied of the other. Thus if the tree is the effect of the seed and cause and effect are identical, although it makes sense to say that the tree is thirty feet tall it is simply false to say that the seed is thirty feet tall. Nāgārjuna therefore concludes that the thesis of the identity of cause and effect is self-contradictory.

Turning now to alternative 2, namely, cause and effect are absolutely different, Nāgārjuna argues as follows: If cause and effect are totally different from each other, what precisely is the relation between the alleged cause and its effect? It is absurd to answer that the relation is causal relation, for that is to beg the question and not to answer it. Any sensible answer to the question should tell us what it means to say that of two different things one is the cause and the other the effect. Unless the reason for calling the one 'cause' and the other 'effect' is given all talk about something being the cause of something else is just babble and word-magic. Nāgārjuna points out that anyone who talks like that must be deluded in thinking that something becomes a cause because he has given it the name 'cause' or an effect because he has given it the name 'effect'. If this were so, we could turn one thing into another merely by calling it a different name.

Further, if the effect is wholly unrelated to the cause, then not only should nothing be able to produce anything, but also anything could be produced from anything — for example, milk from stone and sand from oil. But no one has so produced. The point here is that the view that cause and effect are absolutely different is as sterile and absurd as its antithesis that they are absolutely identical. To put the point more generally, the proponent of the identity-thesis as well as his opponent, the advocate of the difference view, forgets that a relation has two functions: it separates and unites two things. Where there is no separation, there can be no uniting, and *vice versa*. It is only by being unaware of this dual role of relation that men lay dogmatic and absolute claims to one aspect of relation to the exclusion of the other. Such claims, as has been shown, can only lead to absurdities and contradictions.

The third alternative is refuted by merely noting that the refutation of the first and that of the second together constitute the refutation of the third. That is, if the thesis that a thing arises out of itself is absurd and the thesis that it arises out of a not-self is also absurd, then surely it is absurd to say that a thing arises out of both itself and a not-self.

The fourth alternative needs no refutation, for it is itself the abandonment of causality; this is the view that there is no relation of any kind between cause and effect and hence things happen randomly. This does not, however, mean that Nāgārjuna upholds this view. Quite the contrary, he is drawing attention to the fact that the view that things happen randomly is a claim about reality. More importantly, anyone who holds such a view has no right to employ the concepts 'cause' and 'effect'. The point here is that if things happen randomly, then 'cause' and 'effect' are empty and meaningless. As such, to hold the randomness thesis on the one hand and employ the concepts of cause and effect on the other is to contradict oneself. Nāgārjuna thus concludes his critique of causation by saying that "at nowhere and at no time can entities ever exist by originating out of themselves, from other, from both (self-other), or from the lack of causes (i.e., and only)."[8]

The moral of this dialectical criticism of causation (sometimes also called 'origination') is that causes and effects understood in an absolute sense can only lead to contradictions. 'Cause' and 'effect' refer to entities that exist relatively and dependently; but if taken as referring to entities existing independently and unconditionally, these concepts engender absurdities. Another way of saying the same thing is, 'cause' and 'effect' are mutually dependent concepts having different referents in different categorial frameworks.

Nāgārjuna analyzes notions of substance and attribute in a similar manner. Some thinkers advance the thesis that only attributes (qualities, properties) are real and not substance; while others claim the counterthesis, namely, only substance is real and not attributes. But, says Nāgārjuna, without attributes substance cannot be known and without substance attributes cannot exist. Where do attributes exist? Do they exist within or without substance? Here too the dogmatic advocate commits the error of claiming reality exclusively for one or the other of two mutually dependent existents. Where there are no substances there can be no attributes, and *vice versa*. It must be emphasized, however, that in saying that substance and attribute are mutually dependent existents Nāgārjuna is not saying that substance and attribute both exist absolutely and ultimately. What he means by "mutually dependent existents" is that the reality of each is conditioned by that of the other. Neither of them exists absolutely but both exist dependently and relatively. Accordingly, Nāgārjuna warns us against falling victim to the illusion that simply because we have the concepts 'substance' and 'attribute' there are in reality some *independently* existing entities called 'substances' and 'attributes'. Nāgārjuna subjects to similar analyses such other concepts as 'existence' and 'non-existence', 'self' and 'non-self', 'unity' and 'plurality', 'subject' and 'object', 'rest' and 'motion', etc., and concludes that none of these concepts refers to any independent, absolute entities in reality. Taken as mutually dependent concepts, they signify *relative* existents; but if taken as referring to absolute, ultimate, and independent existents, these concepts lead to contradictions and absurdities. Hence one of the deepest insights of *Jñāna-yoga*: If any category of a framework is absolutized, whether explicitly or implicitly, contradiction and falsehood are inevitable and necessary.

I shall now discuss some examples to illustrate the above insight. One of the most ancient of philosophical controversies concerns the question whether ultimate reality is unchanging and eternal or pure flux and change with nothing abiding and enduring. Expressed in terms of categories, the question is whether ultimate reality is substance or process. The view that ultimate reality is one, unchanging substance is known as 'eternalism'; in contrast, the thesis that it is pure change and process is known as 'annihilationism'. Each of these opposing views have had staunch defenders at all times in the intellectual saga of man. We have seen earlier that the pre-Socratic philosophers, Parmenides and Heraclitus, upheld the substance and process views, respectively. According to Heraclitus, ultimate reality is pure flux and change, there being no enduring and eternal entities anywhere; and Parmenides taught that ultimate reality is one, unchanging and eternal. Each of these two philosophers and their followers went on to construct various arguments in defense of their own thesis. Consistent with their theses, Heraclitus held that permanence is an illusion, whereas Parmenides regarded change as illusion. And throughout the history of philosophy,[9] some thinkers have come to be identified as substance-philosophers and others as process-philosophers. Thus Plato, Aristotle, Aquinas, Descartes, Spinoza, Leibniz, and Kant belong to the substance variety; whereas Henri Bergson, John Dewey, and Alfred North Whitehead belong to the process variety. The substance-versus-process controversy goes on unabated in our own day. What went wrong?

'Substance' is defined as the substratum, that which remains unchanged in time; and 'process' is defined as change — flux. It is to be immediately noted that the concept of substance necessarily involves reference to change and process, and that of process necessarily refers to substance. Thus substance is that which remains *unchanged in time*, and process is change that *something* undergoes. It is therefore clear that the concept of substance cannot be understood without change, and that of process cannot be understood without something that undergoes change. This is to say that 'substance' and 'process' are mutually dependent concepts — each deriving its meaning in reference and contrast to the other.

It is an undeniable fact of our experience that permanence and change are equally discernible in the world. It is to be emphasized, however, that the permanence and change that we observe are *relative* permanence and *relative* change. Thus when my friend John Bewilderado points to his writing desk and proudly proclaims that it is the *same* desk his great grandfather, grandfather, and father used, are we to think that there have been no changes in the desk since it was made a century ago? Certainly not; for on inspection we find that the desk had undergone several changes — nicks, dents, warps, discoloration, weakening of the wood, etc. What this means, then, is that the desk is *relatively* permanent, not an absolutely unchanging entity. Likewise, the changes that occurred are *relative* changes, not absolute changes — changes that made the desk vanish away into non-existence. This is precisely what I mean by 'relative permanance' and 'relative change'. We see the object still as desk but with certain changes. That is, 'change' and 'permanence' are categories that are legitimately and appropriately employable for organizing and analyzing our experience and thereby for producing categorial knowledge-claims. Thus even while we are perfectly justified in regarding the desk as a permanent object — a substance — we can only do so by implicitly acknowledging change and process. In a word, the desk is a relatively permanent object, relatively to certain changes. And in a like manner, when we talk about change and process, we can only do so by implicitly acknowledging something that undergoes change; that is, it is relative change, relatively to something that undergoes change. To put it pointedly, bare substance and bare change (process) are inconceivable, unimaginable, and beyond our ken, except as pure abstractions.

Now a given thinker may construct a framework of which 'substance' is a category. This thinker, by employing his framework, makes certain knowledge-claims, such as "X is a substance". This is to say that the thinker acknowledges, through his framework, substances among existents. But, this is the important point, since 'substance' cannot be comprehended and explicated without reference to 'process' ('change'), the framework is sustained by what it claims to exclude. Similar is the case with respect to a framework which includes the category 'change' and excludes 'substance'. It is therefore clear that an inquirer whose framework includes 'substance' cannot use that category to make knowledge-claims, without at the same time recognizing change; likewise, a thinker whose framework includes 'process' cannot employ that category without simultaneously recognizing substance. The point we have made earlier about the tension between the included and the excluded as that which sustains and upholds a framework should now be clear.

But in one's thirst for knowledge of the absolute — which at heart is the quest for being — one forgets that 'substance' and 'process' are mutually dependent categories, neither of which can be absolutized, one goes on to claim that ultimate reality is *exclusively* of the nature of substance or process. That is, the inquirer has absolutized a category of his framework. Such absolutization inevitably lands him in contradiction and absurdity. For how is one to understand the declaration, "ultimate reality is of the essence of substance", when the very meaning and comprehensibility of 'substance' is inseparably bound up with that of 'process'? In a similar manner, how is one to understant the claim, "ultimate reality is pure flux and change", when the very meaning of 'process' is ineluctably bound up with that of 'substance'? Both these claims are the product of the error of absolutizing relative and dependent categories. For, if by 'ultimate reality' one means reality besides which there is none, and substance and change are categorially correlative, then surely the claim that ultimate reality is exclusively substance as well as the claim that ultimate reality is exclusively process is absurd and self-contradictory, and hence false. 'Substance' without 'change' and 'change' without 'substance' are self-contradictory concepts. The crucial mistake, then, is to take perfectly sensible and useful categories from out of frameworks, their natural home, and apply them to ultimate reality.

It follows that 'substance' and 'process' are applicable only in a domain of plurality — a domain in which there are at least one thing (substance) and one change (process). These categories cannot be applied to whatever is construed to be ultimate — one besides which nothing can there be. Substance needs process besides it, and *vice versa*; and hence these categories cannot be applied to ultimate reality without leading to their breakdown, which manifests itself as contradictions. Expressed generally, then, every claim which reads "ultimate reality is ....", where the dotted space is occupied by a category-term is self-contradictory. One who claims that ultimate reality is a categorial thus-and-such inescapably pays the high price of having to regard certain genuine aspects of our experience as illusory. Is it not true that Parmenides, in proclaiming that ultimate reality is one and unchanging, had to declare all change as illusory and unreal? And is it not the case that Heraclitus, in claiming that ultimate reality is pure flux, with nothing abiding, had to relegate permanence to the illusory and the unreal?

To take another example, consider the time-honored philosophic controversy of the physical-versus-mental. Thus on the one hand, there are those who declare that ultimate reality is through and through physical, 'physical' being understood as material — matter in motion; and on the other hand, some thinkers claim that ultimate reality is of the essence of mind. The former are known as 'physicalists' and the latter as 'mentalists'. According to the physicalist, the so-called mental (mind) is nothing but the physical, in particular the neurophysiological; thus thoughts and feelings are merely neurophysiological processes, neuronal movements. In contrast, the mentalist teaches that the so-called matter (the meterial) is nothing but a product of the mind. For the physicalist, the mental is illusory; and for the mentalist, the physical is illusory. It should be clear that each of the warring groups is advancing a *monistic* claim as to what ultimate reality is like, the difference being that one party wants to reduce everything to the physical, while the other wishes to reduce everything to the mental; for, according to one faction, there is nothing besides the physical; and, according to the other, there is nothning besides the mental. And the controversy goes on with undiminished intensity and ferocity. It is not my purpose here, however, to discuss in detail the various solutuions proposed to the problem of the physical-versus-mental.[10] Suffice it to establish that the problem and the debate have their genesis in a grave error, which itself is the result of the thirst for knowledge of the absolute, the unconditioned, and the ultimate.

'Physical' and 'mental' are first and foremost categories of frameworks we construct in light of our experience. It is an indisputable fact that there are two clearly distinguishable modes of our experience — our experience of tables, chairs, stones, stars, etc. on the one hand, and our experience of thoughts, emotions, feelings, images, dreams, etc. on the other. In other words, we experience, *as a matter of fact,* the physical in a manner different from that in which we experience the mental. It is extremely important to note that neither the physical nor the mental comes to us with labels such as 'real', 'illusory', or 'unreal'. That is, in itself there is nothing about the physical or the mental by which we can claim it to be real, illusory, or unreal. Do we experience thoughts and feelings as any the less real than sticks and stones? Is our dream-experience less real than our waking experience, for example, my seeing a lamp on my desk now? If so, how, in what manner, and by what criteria does one come to claim the one as real and ultimate and the other as unreal, non-ultimate, or illusory? And what precisely does one mean by saying that the one is reducible — without residuum — to the other? Is it not true that when we dream what is dreamt is experienced as real, as witness people waking up in cold sweat, with their hearts racing? When we dream, the waking world, the world of waking experience, is non-existent, just as when we are awake the dream-world is non-existent. It is only on waking up that one says to oneself, "well, that was just a dream", and goes on to declare it as unreal and illusory. What this means, then, is that there are no signs, no marks, no criteria within waking experience or dream-experience itself by which to pronounce which is real and which unreal, whether the dream-world or the world of waking experience. May it not be that simply because we spend considerably more time awake than asleep and dreaming, we tend to think that the world of waking experience is real and that of dream-experience unreal? In order to appreciate this point, just imagine what it would be like if we were the kind of beings who spent the greater part of their lives sleeping and dreaming rather than awake. Would we not then consider the world of waking experience unreal and that of dream-experience real? It should be clear from all these considerations that we arbitrarily post the sign 'reality' in one domain, say the waking world, and then go on to proclaim that the other, the world of dream-experience, is illusory and unreal (and *vice versa*). Without first affixing such a label, the signpost, there is no basis on which to regard the one or the other of the worlds as real or unreal. To put it differently, the world of waking experience and that of dream-experience form a continuum, there being no *self-given* criteria in either of them by which to consider the one as real and the other unreal and illusory.

The upshot of all the above considerations, then, is that the physical and the mental have equal claim to reality, since, as a matter of fact, they are both clearly distinguishable and equally genuine modes of our experience. Thus if I ask you now to imagine, for example, the Eiffel tower, and after a few seconds you say, "Yes, what next?" am I to understand you as saying that your experience of the image of the Eiffel tower is an experience of something unreal and non-existent? Nothing could be more preposterous, for you surely mean that your experience is that of a mental image, not of sheer nothing or something unreal and non-existent. For, in the first place, how could anything unreal be an object of our experience? You also acknowledge that your experience of the image is as genuine as your experience of, say, your watch; you further grant that your experience of the watch is distinguishable from your experience of the image of the Eiffel tower. For one thing, the watch can be assigned *both* spatial and temporal co-ordinates, whereas the image can be assigned *only* a temporal co-ordinate but not a spatial one; that is, it cannot be said to be in space, at least the kind of space in which the so-called physical objects are said to be. But does such a difference make the one real and the other unreal and illusory? The answer is definitely in the negative.

It is to be noted that 'physical' and 'mental' are mutually dependent and relative categories. That is, each derives its meaning in contrast with the other. As such, neither can be absolutized without contradiction and absurdity. Let me now clearly point out this absurdity.

If, as claimed by the physicalist, everything is physical, what could he possibly mean by 'physical'? He could just as well have called it 'glibzectal'. This is to say that the claim that everything is physical — ultimate reality is physical — cannot be understood if we have no experience of the mental, the non-physical. It is only because we also have the experience of the mental, we understand what it is to say that something is physical. If every object in the world is, for example, what we now call 'red', what difference would it make if instead of 'red' we use the word 'blue' (or, for that matter, any nonsense word such as 'zmlu')? None whatever. One mistakenly believes that one's claim that ultimate reality is physical makes sense, only by being oblivious to the fact that the concept of the physical has, in the first place, its origins in our experience of the non-physical (the mental). Thus one starts out employing the category 'physical' by deriving its meaning from one's experiential contrast with the mental, and then in one's thirst for knowledge of the absolute one ignorantly, illegitimately, and dogmatically tries to banish away the category of the mental, by proclaiming that everything is physical — ultimate reality is physical. But once one of the categories is banished away, the other ceases to be meaningful and becomes empty. Hence the claim that everything is physical, as well as the claim that everything is mental, is insane and absurd. As for the contradiction, here is how it arises: On the one hand the claim that everything is physical aims at abolishing the category of the mental, and yet on the other hand, for the claim to make sense, it *must* refer to the very category it aims to liquidate. And one simply cannot have it both ways. Hence the contradiction. And since ultimate reality, by one's own definition, is reality besides which there is none, what sense does it make to categorize it, whether as physical or mental? None at all, because categorization is sensible, legitimate, appropriate, and beneficial only in a domain consisting of at least two *kinds* of phenomenon, whatever they may be. This means that plurality of kind is a necessary condition for the very emergence of categories and hence for categorization itself. Where there is no plurality of type (kind), categorization is senseless and absurd. Thus in advancing the claim that ultimate reality is subsumable under a certain category, whatever it may be, one is at the same time denying that it is ultimate reality; thence arises the contradiction. This again shows that every claim that reads, "ultimate reality is ....", where the dotted space is filled by a category-term, necessarily leads to contradiction and absurdity. It is worth noting in this context that there are many religions in which ultimate reality is described variously as person, spirit, creator, father, etc. And it should be evident, in light of the foregoing analysis, that these religious characterizations are also absurd and self-contradictory. For is it not true that the categories 'person', 'spirit', etc. derive their meanings from our experiential contrast with non-person and non-spirit? If so, how can they be absolutized without doing serious violence to the very rationality which makes categories possible?

We therefore conclude that it is one of the most radical and profound insights of *Jñāna-yoga* that ultimate reality is uncharacterizable by any category, no matter how lofty and sublime its meaning may be. And if one ignorantly and dogmatically claims a categorial description of ultimate reality, one pays the exorbitant price of contradiction and absurdity, the very breakdown of reason itself. This is the same as saying that all categories are relative and dependent, and serve us well only insofar as we wisely and skillfully employ them dependently and relatively to arrive at universal truths, which are not absolute but relative truths ("relative truth" does not mean falsehood). And if a category is uprooted from its native soil — a categorial framework — and used to make absolute claims, contradiction, absurdity, and falsehood are inevitable. Thus every brand of metaphysics, insofar as it lays absolute claims on behalf of some categorial claim, is necessarily dogmatic and is undoubtedly the product of ignorance — lack of insight into the very means by which we produce knowledge-claims.

Before proceeding further with the discussion of categories and categorial frameworks, I shall discuss another fundamental insight of *Jñāna-yoga*.

The Principle of Dependent Origination:[11] This principle is also known as "The Principle of Co-production". Although this extraordinary and penetrating insight is contained in the Upaniṣadic teachings, it was first stated most explicitly by the Buddha and is generally regarded as the most profound finding resulting from his Enlightenment. Simply stated, it is as follows: this phenomenon arising, that phenomenon arises; and this phenomenon ceasing to be, that phenomenon ceases to be. One can easily find detailed treatments of this principle in standard works on Buddhist philosophy.[12] We are concerned here, however, with its deep and broad-ranging significance to the way of knowledge — *Jñāna-yoga* — and the implications thereof. For this reason, I shall treat this topic in some detail.

The Principle of Dependent Origination is first and foremost a statement as to the essential trait of the entire world of phenomena — things, events, processes, properties, relations, etc. And what is a phenomenon? A phenomenon is anything whatever that is (or can be) either in both space and time or just in time. Thus the so-called physical objects are *both* in space and time; whereas thoughts, emotions, and feelings — briefly, the psychological, the non-physical — are *only* in time. But if someone wants to claim that thoughts and feelings are also in space, he should grant us this much: whatever space it is in which thoughts and feelings are supposed to exist, it is not the same kind of space in which physical objects are said to exist. And for our purposes the nature of the space, if any, inhabited by thoughts and feelings is irrelevant and inconsequential. The essential point here is that physical objects as well as psychological objects — thoughts, emotions, and feelings — whatever they may be, are all equally phenomena, insofar as they are all time-bound existents; and to exist in time is to be subject to change, and to be subject to change is to arise and pass away. Arising and passing away, then, are the hallmark of all phenomena.

How does a phenomenon arise (come to be)? And how does it pass away? According to the Principle of Dependent Origination, every phenomenon arises in dependence upon other phenomena and passes away in dependence upon other phenomena. Put differently, no phenomenon can arise by itself — on its own — or pass away by itself; it is only in dependence upon other phenomena that a given phenomenon can arise and pass away. The reader may now consider any phenomenon and verify for himself the truth of the above declaration.

To say that every phenomenon arises and passes away in dependence on other phenomena is to say that no phenomenon is self-existent or has self-nature. Since every phenomenon owes its existence and nature, whatever it may be, to other phenomena, every phenomenon is bereft of own-existence and own-nature. Thus, for example, a tree, which is a pehnomenon, has no existence or nature apart from other phenomena, such as the seed, water, sunshine, etc. And just as a tree comes into existence in dependence upon other phenomena, so also it passess away in dependence upon other phenomena — as when it is consumed by a forest-fire. Such is the case with respect to all phenomena, without exception. Hence the following alternative statement of the Principle of Dependent Origination: All phenomena are wholly devoid of own-existence and own-nature (*svabhāva-śūnya-dharma*). There can be nothing in the entire world of phenomena which has own-existence or own-nature. This is precisely what is meant by saying that all phenomena are *empty*, empty of self-existence and self-nature. Let it be emphasized that 'empty' here does not mean non-existence or lack of nature; rather, it means lack of own-existence and own-nature. It is in this sense that all phenomena are empty.

It is clear from the foregoing that every phenomenon is a dependent and relative existent, and has a dependent and relative nature. Consequently, the concept of a pehenomenon as an absolute and independent existent, with an absolute and independent nature, is a contradiction in terms. That is, nothing with self-existence and self-nature can ever be found in the phenomenal world, time-bound existence. Only the unreflective and the uncritical think and claim that some pehenomenon is self-existent and has a self-nature. A moment's reflection reveals that to say that some phenomenon is self-existent and has a self-nature is to say that the phenomenon is untouched, unaffected, and uninfluenced by other phenomena. But since it is an undeniable truth that all phenomena exist in time, a self-existent, whatever it may be, cannot, in principle, be in time. In brief, the self-existent is not and cannot be a phenomenon. To sum up, no phenomenon is a self-existent and no self-existent is a phenomenon. Thus, X is a phenomenon if and only if X is not a self-existent, which is but a compact way of saying that if X is a phenomenon, then X is not a self-existent *and* if X is not a self-existent, then X is a phenomenon. It is of the highest importance to note that the question whether or not there is (or can be) a self-existent has no bearing whatever on the truth of the Principle of Dependent Origination. For the principle is a declaration of the truth concerning the nature of phenomena — the phenomenal world — to the effect that all phenomena are devoid of self-existence and self-nature, and *not* about whether or not there is (or can be) a self-existent.

I shall now inquire into the relation between the Principle of Dependent Origination and that of superimposition. The former is a statement about the pervasive and fundamental trait of the world of phenomena; and it is essential to realize that this statement could not have been made were it not for the Principle of Superimposition. This means that without the categories 'phenomenon', 'dependence', and 'origination' the Principle of

Dependent Originagion cannot in the first place be formulated. Simply put, the Principle of Superimposition is the necessary condition for the Principle of Dependent Origination. It is through superimposition, central to which is the sundering apart of unitary experience into the perceiver and the perceived —.subject and object — that the above categories, like all other categories, are first formed, and then by employing them one formulates the Principle of Dependent Origination. For this reason, the principle is best construed as pertaining first to categories and then *via* categories to their referents,[13] namely, phenomena. I am not hereby implying that one cannot have a category for which there is no phenomenal referent; but then the category is just a word, a pure abstraction, having nothing to do with our experience and knowledge, actual or possible. Consequently, whoever claims such a category must grant that it refers to a self-existent, which, in principle, cannot be a phenomenon. And just as an absolutized category can bear no relation to another category, so also a supposed self-existent is totally isolated from all phenomena — in a word, a self-existent is no part of the world of phenomena. We have shown earlier in this chapter that all categories are relative and mutually dependent, which means that no category can have any meaning or referent apart from another category. Each category gains meaning by virtue of its contrast with another category. Thus, from the point of view of production of knowledge — knowing the world — there is on the part of the knowing subject the activity of superimposition, which is none other than the production of a network of categories, under which to subsume, organize, and analyze our experience of the world; and in this manner, one projects, as it were, the categorial nexus onto the plane of experience and thereby claims that the world of our experience is a world of *phenomena*. And since the categorial network is through and through one of mutuality and relativity, its projection, namely the world of our experience — the world of phenomena — is also one of mutual dependence and relativity. Thus the genesis of the Principle of Dependent Origination, as a statement pertaining to the world of phenomena, is to be found in the Principle of Dependent Origination, as a statement pertaining to categories and categorial frameworks; and this latter statement is none other than the statement of the product of the activity of superimposition on the part of the inquirer. This, then, is the full meaning of my contention that the Principle of Superimposition is the necessary condition for the Principle of Dependent Origination; and there should be nothing surprising about this, for is it not the case that without superimposition there can be no talk of knowledge-claims? It needs to be emphasized that the Principle of Dependent Origination is a knowledge-claim at Level 3, and all beings constructed as we — human beings — are certify that the world of our experience is a world of phenomena, that every phenomenon arises and passes away in dependence upon other phenomena, and that all phenomena exist in time, while some also exist in space.

Since, as demonstrated above, the Principle of Dependent Origination is a fundamental knowledge-claim at Level 3, it is most fittingly regarded as one of the pillars of *Jñāna-yoga*. It is not important that the reader agree with my conclusion concerning the above characterization of the Principle of Dependent Origination and its truth; rather, what is important is that he critically examine the analyses and arguments and determine for himself the veracity or otherwise of my claim on behalf of the principle. I shall conclude this part of our discussion by exhibiting in a juxtapositional format the projective relationship between the Principle of Superimposition and that of Dependent Origination (see the table below).

The Principle of Dependent Origination

as pertaining to categories	*as pertaining to phenomena*
1. Category	Phenomenon
2. No category in and by itself can have meaning or referent.	No phenomenon can arise or pass away by itself.
3. Category A depends for its meaning and referent	Phenomenon P arises or passes away in dependence upon some

	on another category, say B.	other phenomena, say Q and R.
4.	Absolutized category	Self-existent and self-nature
5.	Absolutization of a category leads to contradiction and absurdity	Absolutization of a phenomenon results in its being regarded as a *non*-phenomenon.
6.	Categories are mutually dependent and relative	Phenomena are mutually dependent and relative.
7.	Nexus of categories	Nexus of phenomena

I turn now to a consideration of the topic of justification of categorial frameworks. It is only to be expected that every inquirer who constructs a categorial framework feels the need to justify his framework by advancing arguments in defense of it. The task of justifying a categorial framework is known as "transcendental deduction of categories", a term originally due to Immanuel Kant.[14] Providing a transcendental deduction for a categorial framework consists of two tasks: (1) showing that as a matter of fact people employ the framework for producing objective knowledge-claims about the world; and (2) showing that it (the framework) is the *only* framework suitable for arriving at objective truths about the world. This latter demonstration is known as "uniqueness demonstration". It is obvious that the former task is easy and straightforward, for it consists of merely ascertaining that people use the framework for their inquiry into and investigation of the world. In contrast, the uniqueness demonstration — showing that the framework is the *only* one which enables one to produce objective knowledge-claims about the world — is fraught with difficulties which are, in principle, impossible to surmount. These difficulties, as will be seen presently, stem from the very nature of a categorial framework, that is, of any categorial framework in general.

Let us assume that a certain thinker has constructed a categorial framework for which he has to offer transcendental deduction. It is not enough for him to show that none of the existing and competing frameworks is inadequate to produce objective knowledge-claims about the world; he needs to show that no framework other than his own, whether in the past, present, or future, can, in principle, be adquate for an objective inquiry into the world. Only then can he be said to have shown that it is impossible for any framework, past, present, or future, other than his own, to be well-suited to an objective study of the world. But how can the thinker accomplish this task? Does he have knowledge of *all* frameworks, past, present, and future, in light of which he has scrutinized them and found them inadequate as instruments of inquiry for enabling one to produce objective knowledge-claims about the world? Certainly not, for how can he have knowledge of all frameworks, past, present, and future? As a matter of fact, he may be, as is often the case, ignorant of even some past and present frameworks. The inescapable conclusion, then, is that the thinker cannot, in principle, accomplish this demonstration. And even if we assume that he has succeeded in this task, he has yet to show that his own framework serves the purpose of producing objective knowledge about the world. In order to show this, he should show that the world is indeed as described by his framework. It is a supreme insight of *Jñāna-yoga* that the thinker cannot, in principle, establish this, and every argument to establish it is necessarily (inevitably) circular and therefore question-begging and fruitless. For in order to demonstrate that the world is as described by his own framework, the thinker needs to know what the world is like independently of his framework, and then show that his framework does indeed describe the world faithfully. And he who understands the profound significance of the Principle of Superimposition realizes that one cannot, in principle, know what the world is like apart from some framework or other, and therefore uniqueness demonstrations are simply impossible. For is it not true that if I showed you a photograph and asked whether it is a picture of my friend Johan Nixmind, you cannot answer unless yōu have seen him at least once? Just so, unless one knows what the world is like independently of categorial frameworks, one cannot sensibly claim that the world is indeed as described by the framework. It is possible that you may have seen Johan Nixmind, but it is certainly impossible for you or anyone else to know what the world is like apart from some framework or other. And for this reason, every argument the inquirer constructs for demonstrating the uniqueness-claim necessarily employs the categories of the very framework (for, on his own admission, there is none else), which in the first place needs justification. The incontrovertible conclusion, then, is that transcendental deductions are impossible and circular.

It is a ringing testimony to the attachment — clinging — born of ignorance, to their own categorial frameworks, that innumerable thinkers down through the ages, our own included, offered transcendental deductions, and Kant himself is no exception to this observation. These remarks are not intended to belittle or denigrate these thinkers; they only serve to underscore the fact that even astute minds are not exempt from succumbing to ignorance, illusion, and attachment.

I come now to the third fundamental insight of *Jñāna-yoga*, namely, the Principle of Two Truths. But before presenting this principle, it is important that we distinguish between reality and a *view* of reality (*dṛṣṭi*). Let us ask: what is the purpose for which a thinker constructs a categorial framework? The purpose of a categorial framework is to enable the thinker to formulate a coherent account of his experience of the world of phenomena. Such an account is indeed a theory, a view of reality; and different categorial frameworks give rise to different views — theories — of reality. We have hitherto established that a view of reality, insofar as it is inextricably bound up with some framework or other, cannot be absolutized without contradiction and absurdity. A view of reality, then, is a system of knowledge-claims, everyone of which is a categorial claim; and every categorial claim is about some phenomenon, some facet of our experience.

But, in his thirst for knowledge of the absolute and the unconditioned, each thinker mistakenly identifies reality with his own *view* of reality; and, as a consequence, he goes on to lay absolute claims for his own view of reality, thus falling into contradiction and absurdity; and in this manner, he inevitably become blind, dogmatic, and intolerant.

It is extremely important to realize, then, that reality is

neither a view nor a collection of views. Reality simply is; it is neither true nor false, neither good nor evil. It is only views of reality that can properly be said to be true or false. Reality is not a knowledge-claim, whereas every view of reality is a knowledge-claim or a system of knowledge-claims. It is instructive to note that these same observations hold with respect to phenomena; thus, for example, the tree in the yard simply is,[15] and is neither true nor false. Only views — knowledge-claims — about the tree can be said to be true or false (of course from within a given categorial framework). In light of these remarks, we shall now proceed to discuss the Principle of Two Truths.

The Principle of Two Truths: The oldest recorded statement of this principle is to be found in the *Muṇḍaka-Upaniṣad*.[16] And in the writings of Nāgārjuna and Śaṅkara it had been fully developed and elaborated upon. According to this principle, there are two kinds of knowledge and truth: (1) the relative, conditioned, mundane, conventional truth — the lower truth (called *saṁvṛtti-satya* as well as *vyāvahārika-satya*); and (2) the absolute, unconditioned, supramundane truth — the higher truth (known as *paramārtha-satya*). We shall briefly refer to these as *saṁvṛtti* and *paramārtha,* respectively. We have shown in our discussion of categorial frameworks that every truth generatable through a categorial framework is necessarily realtive, conditioned, and conventional, in the sense that the truth arises from and is subject to the conventions — categories, definitions, rules, and principles — of the framework and is about some segement of the world of phenomena. Put differently, all categorial truths are perceptual-conceptual truths; they are relative, in that if they are absolutized one is led into contradiction and absurdity; they are conditioned, in that each category depends for its meaning and referent upon — is conditioned by — other categories; the truths are mundane, in the sense that they are about the world of phenomena, the world of the senses and intellect. The truths declared by the various branches of empirical science, such as physics, chemistry, biology, psychology, economics, as well as those proclaimed by formal sciences, such as logic and mathematics, are all unexceptionally lower truths. Lower truths are open to inspection and certification by formal and empirical procedures by all inquirers who are constituted alike and operate with a given categorial framework . This is to say that the last court of appeal for accepting or rejecting lower truths is formal-empirical certifiability and pragmatic efficacy.

In sharp contrast, the higher truth — *paramārtha* — is non-categorial, non-phenomenal, non-perceptual, and non-conceptual. As such, the higher truth is absolute, unconditioned, and supramundane. It cannot be grasped through any categorial framework; that is, it transcends the senses and intellect. Whereas every lower truth is a *view* of reality (or an integral component of a view of reality), the higher truth is not a view of reality at all. It follows, then, that while lower truths are grasped through the senses and intellect — categorial frameworks — the higher truth is to be apprehended non-perceptually and non-conceptually, that is, non-categorially, directly, and intuitively. Another way characterizing the distinction between lower truths and the higher truth is to note that conflict and opposition can only arise between one lower truth and another, but not between a lower truth and the higher truth — as witness the perennial antagonism among several views of reality: physicalism-versus-mentalism, materialism-versus-spiritualism, and so on. The higher truth cannot conflict with any lower truth, because, the former, not being a product of perception and conception, is non-categorial; whereas the latter is always and inevitably categorial. Rality, itself not being a view, is therefore fully compatible with *all* views. It is worth noting in this context that, whereas other thinkers only distinguish between the rational and the irrational, the *Jñāna-yogin* distinguishes the rational, irrational, and the non-rational. The attributes 'rational' and 'irrational' pertain to categorial — lower — truths only. Thus, for example, when one holds up an object and says, "this is a flower", and someone else counters, "that is a stone", the two claims conflict with each other. To say that the claim that the object is a flower is rational is to say that different inquirers, who are all constituted alike and who conduct their inquiry with a given framework, will certify that claim to be true; consequently, they will all declare that the claim that the object is a stone is irrational. But irrational in what sense? The claim is regarded as irrational in the sense that the person who makes that claim is either ignorant of the meanings and referents of 'flower' and 'stone', as delineated in the framework of his opponents, or that his sense-organs are defective in that he sees flowers as stones. We are of course not interested in the sterile debate that what one calls a 'flower' the other calls a 'stone'. The crucial point here is that for the two claims to contradict each other it is necessary that both parties operate with categorial frameworks. This is to say that 'rational' and 'irrational' both pertain to categorial knowledge-claims; which is the same as saying that the rational and the irrational are equally within the purview of categorial frameworks and hence of categorial knowledge; for otherwise, they cannot be in opposition. In keen contrast, the non-rational is wholly, fully, and totally outside of any categorial framework and categorial knowledge. All of this may be expressed by saying that it is only of *views* of reality that one can sensibly and appropriately say that they are rational or irrational. Reality, itself, *not* being a view, alongside other views, is non-rational. It simply is.

To sum up, then, every lower truth is rational or irrational, from the standpoint of some categorial framework or other. The higher truth, lying entirely outside the scope of all categorial frameworks, actual or possible, is through and through non-rational; consequently, it cannot be certified by any categorial procedure. Rather, it is to be apprehended by a total suspension of the very means by which categorial frameworks are produced in the first place, namely, perception and conception, which are the warp and woof of the mundane and the phenomenal. It should be clear by now that bringing to total cessation all perceptual-conceptual activity is necessary for the experience of the higher truth. This in turn means that the cessation of the activity of superimposition is the necessary condition for the experience of the higher truth. We shall discuss later how to bring about such a cessation. Suffice it for now to emphasize that all lower truths, without exception, are capable of linguistic expression; and in contrast, the higher truth, transcending all perceptions and conceptions, is inexpressible and incommunicable. And if someone attempts to express the higher truth, he inevitably has to resort to some categorial framework and will thereby end up by proclaiming a lower truth — as witness the plethora of claims such as: reality is matter in motion, reality is person, reality is mind, reality is spirit, and so on. Nothing brings out this point more clearly than the notorious fact of religious animosity and antagonism. For is it not true that more than anything else it is religions, minor or major, that make absolute claims as to what reality is? Almost every religion is guilty of the grievous error of ignorantly mistaking a lower truth for the higher truth, and the result, needless to say, is dogmatism, intolerance, and zealotry, in whose wake follow unspeakable forms of horror, cruelty, and inhumanity.

When one of the supreme masters, Lao Tze, teaches that he who knows the Tao — Reality — does not speak of It, and he who speaks of the Tao does not know It,[17] he bears witness to the profound and inexpressible character of the higher truth. Lao Tze thus confirms the deepest insight of *Jñāna-yoga* into the higher knowledge and truth — *paramārtha*. Notice that Lao Tze does not talk about a *view* of the Tao as inexpressible and incommunicable; rather, he talks of the Tao Itself, the non-rational, as inexpressible and incommunicable. Like the *Muṇḍaka-Upaniṣad*, Lao Tze gives a pithy expression to his insight into the higher truth; and the great *Jñāna-yogins*, Nāgārjuna and Śaṅkara, establish, through systematic and unrelenting inquiry and analyses, the inexpressibility and incommunicability of the higher truth. Every walker of the way of knowledge is indebted to these illustrious masters of the path.

It is the thirst for the real and the absolute, which is but the quest for being, that makes people oblivious to the distinction *Jñāna-yoga* makes between lower truths and the higher truth (*saṃvṛtti* and *paramārtha*, respectively). It should abundantly be clear by now that this distinction can only be captured through thoroughgoing and uncompromising inquiry into the nature of categorial frameworks and categorial knowledge in general. It deserves to be emphasized that lower truths are many and varied, whereas there is one, and only one, higher truth. This should not be surprising, for lower truths pertain to the phenomenal world, which is paradigmatic of plurality. Is it any wonder, then, that there are many (plurality of) lower truths? A lower truth, by its very nature, that is, being categorial, is one among many. In contrast, the higher truth, being wholly uncategorial, can only be one; for is it not the case that there is but one reality, while there are many *views* of reality? One might ask now: how many views of reality can there be? Answer: In light of our analysis and discussion of categorial frameworks, there can be as many views of reality as there are beings capable of constructing views of reality (this is minimally so, for a single being can construct more than one view). Just think of the variety and multiplicity of views of reality advocated and embraced by human beings, the kind of beings capable of producing views of reality and inhabiting this planet, an infinitesimal segment of the vast cosmos, you will see the truth of this answer. Thus the relation between reality and views of reality can correctly be characterized as a one-many relation. We shall bring this chapter to a close by a summary of the three seminal insights of *Jñāna-yoga*: The Principle of Superimposition, The Principle of Dependent Origination, and The Principle of Two Truths.

1. *The Principle of Superimposition*: This principle calls attention to the activity of superimposition — the imposition of names and forms — on the part of the inquirer in the production of knowledge of the world of phenomena, the world of the senses and intellect. To understand this principle is to realize that production of knowledge is not a passive registration of data by the inquirer; rather, it is the dynamic process of the inquirer's active role in the organization and analysis of his experience of some sector or other of the world of phenomena. Consequently, the knowledge and truths an inquirer claims about the world inevitably and unmistakably bear his stamp; for, after all, what is human knowledge? It is knowledge that is produced by human-beings — beings of a certain psycho-physiological constitution. It follows that the notion of objective knowledge and objective truth, as knowledge and truth which have nothing whatever to do with the kind of beings who claim them, is the grossest of superstitions. Objective knowledge and objective

truth are no more and no less than knowledge and truth producible and certifiable by all inquirers of a certain type of constitution who conduct their inquiry with a given superimpositional — categorial — framework.

2. *The Principle of Dependent Origination:* This principle is the insight that every phenomenon arises and passes away in dependence upon other phenomena. The world of phenomena is thus through and through time-bound. This is the same as saying that change and dynamism are the very being of the world of phenomena. To say that every phenomenon arises and passes away in dependence upon other phenomena is to say that no phenomenon is self-existent or has self-nature. That is, the existence as well as the nature of a phenomenon is dependent upon other phenomena. Hence, there can be nothing in the world of phenomena which has own-existence or own-nature. This is not to be construed, however, as saying that phenomena are devoid of existence or nature; rather, they lack *own*-existence and *own*-nature. For is it not true that bread nourishes us while stones do not? If bread and stones do not have their natures, why do we not feed ourselves stones? The point, then, is that given the kind of beings we are, bread nourishes us and stones do not. Let us therefore emphasize that the human being, bread, and stones all have each an existence and a nature, but not own-existence and own-nature. It is presicely the lack of own-existence and own-nature that is signalled by the declaration that all phenomena are *empty*. Self-existence and self-natures — absolute existents and absolute natures — cannot be integral components of the world of phenomena. It is due to ignorance of this profound truth concerning pehnomena that people mistakenly regard some phenomenon as absolute and attribute to it properties that can only properly be predicated of phenomena. The ineluctable consequence of such ignorance is contradiction, absurdity, and dogmatism.

3. *The Principle of Two Truths:* This principle is the teaching that knowledge and truth are of two kinds: the lower and the higher. Lower truths are relative, conditioned, mundane, and conventional; they pertain to phenomena; that is, every lower

truth is a perceptual-conceptual truth and is hence inseparably bound up with some superimpositional—categorial—framework or other. For this reason, no lower truth can be absolutized without the peril of contradiction and absurdity. It is important to see the connection between the fact of the dependent (relative) existence and nature of phenomena and that of the relative nature of lower truths. If phenomena are relative and dependent, it is only to be expected that the truths concerning them will also be relative and dependent. Furthermore, since the world of phenomena is one of plurality, the domain of lower truths is also a realm of plurality. Put differently, there is a multiplicity of phenomena and there is a variety of lower truths, whose truth or falsity is determinable through formal-empirical procedures by inquirers of similar psycho-physiological constitution and who conduct their investigation with a given categorial framework.

In contradistinction, the higher truth is non-perceptual and non-conceptual — in a word, non-categorial. The higher truth cannot therefore be captured in any categorial framework, but can only be experienced in direct, non-dual intuition (*prajñā*) arising from the cessation of perceptual-conceptual activity. In other words, the cessation of the activity of superimposition is the necessary prerequisite for the experience of the higher truth.

The distinction between lower truths and the higher truth arises from discerning the primordial distinction between reality and *views* of reality. Reality is not a view or system of views. Reality simply is; and, not being a view alongside other views, reality is neither true nor false. Accordingly, the adjectives 'rational' and 'irrational' are properly attributable only to views but not to reality which is non-rational. This means that reality as the non-rational transcends the province of the rational and the irrational. This is to be expected, for the rational and the . irrational are wholly within the purview of percepts and concepts. This is the same as saying that the higher truth transcends the senses and intellect, that is, transcends all categorial frameworks. Not being one among several views, reality is compatible with *all* views, rational as well as irrational. As such, conflict and opposition can only be between one view and another, but not between reality and a view. In order to further illuminate this point, we may analogically (and only analogically) speak of reality as space. And what is the great virtue of space? The great and singular virtue of space consists of its ability to accommodate all objects equanimously. But how is space able to do this? Space is able to accommodate all objects equanimously because it is itself not an object among other objects. Opposition and resistance can only arise between one object and another, but not between space and any object. Just so, reality, itself not being a view, is in full harmony with any and all views.

Let it be emphasized that whereas lower truths are many and sundry, there is but one higher truth. The fact of the plurality of lower truths is but the epistemological reflection of the existential fact of the plurality of phenomena. And the fact that there is one, and only one, higher truth is but the consequence of there being a sole and single reality.

To mistake a lower truth, no matter how attractive, compelling, and sublime, for the higher truth is a product of ignorance (*avidyā*). Such ignorance has grave consequences; for not only does it lead to contradiction and absurdity but breeds dogmatism, intolerance, and utter blindness, which are but the fountainhead of pain, suffering, and ill-being in general. The welter of absolute claims on behalf of some lower truth or other, as can easily be gathered from even a cursory examination of the intellectual and religious history of man, is a resounding but tragic testimony to the high cost of his ignorant and obdurate attempts to turn a lower truth into the higher truth. *Jñāna-yoga* is the antidote to this ancient and pervasive poison of ignorance.

Notes

1. For an excellent techincal discussion of categorial frameworks, *see* Stephan Körner, *Categorial Frameworks,* Barnes & Noble, New York, 1970.

2. *The Vedānta Sūtras of Bādarāyaṇa, with Commentary by Śaṅkara,* tr. by George Thibaut, 2 Vols., Dover, New York, 1970.

3. *Nāgārjuna: A Translation of his Mūla-madhyamaka-kārikā, with an Introductory Essay,* by K. Inada, Hokuseido Press, Tokyo, 1970.

4. *See The Vedānta-Sūtras;* also Paul Deussen's *The System of the Vedānta,* tr. by Charles Johnston, Dover, New York, 1973. For a clear and concise treatment of Śaṅkara's *Vedānta, see* Eliot Deutsch's *Advaita-Vedānta: A Philosophical Reconstruction,* East-West Center Press, Honolulu, 1969.

5. For an illuminating and masterful treatment of the topic of shifts in frameworks, *see* Thomas S. Kuhn's *The Structures of Scientific Revolutions,* Second Edition, University of Chicago Press, Chicago, 1970.

6. *See* Thomas Kuhn's *The Structure of Scientific Revolutions,* Second Edition, University of Chicago Press, Chicago, 1970.

7. *Nāgārjuna: A Translation of His Mūla-madhyamaka-kārikā, with an Introductory Essay,* by Kenneth K. Inada, The Hokuseido Press, Tokyo, 1970.

8. *Mūla-madhyamaka-kārikā,* I. 1.

9. *See* Copleston, F., *A History of Philosophy,* 8 vols., Doubleday, Garden City, New York.

10. For a detailed examination of this problem, *see* R Puligandla, *An Encounter with Awareness,* Quest Books, Wheaton, Illinois, 1981, pp. 51-104.

11. *Pratītya-samut-pāda,* in Sanskrit.

12. *See,* for instance, K. N. Jayatilleke, *Early Buddhist Theory of Knowledge,* George Allen & Unwin, London, 1963.

13. 'referent' means anything that is referred to by a symbol; categories are symbols and therefore have referents, either physical or non-physical.

14. Kant, *Critique of Pure Reason,* tr. by N.K. Smith, St. Martin's Press, New York, 1965, pp. 120-75.

15. It is of course true that whether or not what one perceives in the yard is to be called a 'tree' is itself dependent upon a categorial framework. But the point here is that whatever one might want to call it, it simply is and is neither true nor false, neither rational nor irrational.

16. *Muṇḍaka-Upaniṣad,* I. i. 4-6.

17. For a masterful translation of Lao Tze's *Tao Te Ching,* with illuminating commentary, *see* Arthur Waley's *The Way and Its Power: A Study of the Tao Te Ching and Its Place in Chinese Thought,* Grove Press, New York, 1958.

3

Implications and Significance

In the last chapter, I have discussed in considerable detail the three fundamental insights of *Jñāna-yoga*. In the present one, I propose to draw out certain implications of these insights and discuss their significance to a deeper and wider understanding of *Jñāna-yoga*. The understanding becomes deeper on clearly seeing the veracity of the various implications of the central insights; and it is at once enhanced in breadth and scope by discerning the unfailing applicability of the implications across a wide range of human experience and knowledge. It is to be noted that the implications are phenomenological-analytical truths. They are phenomenological in the sense that they are grounded in our direct — unmediated by any theory or instrumentation — experiential base; consequently, their truth cannot be certified without appealing to this experiential — phenomenological — base. These truths are also analytical, in that they cannot be denied without self-contradiction.

A superficial thinker will be tempted to regard some, perhaps all, of the implications to be considered as tautologous — empty and uninformative statements. Here a word of explanation is in order. Yes, the implications are tautologous but are *not* empty statements. How so? *Jñāna-yoga* requires the one who claims that the implications are tautologous and empty to tell us how in the first place he came to certify then to be tautologous and empty; and when one inquires into the process by which one comes to see and declare them as tautologous, one acknowledges that they are not empty statements but fundamental truths about the very structure of our experience. What makes them tautologous — analytical — is the fact that we first dissect the experience pertaining to a statement and then give expression to that experience in precisely those categories by which it has originally been dissected. This is the source and foundation of the tautologousness of the essential insights and their implications. We shall inquire later in detail into the question as to the sense in which the three fundamental insights of *Jñāna-yoga* as well as their implications are said to be true. Suffice it for now to emphasize that there are certain insights which stem from the very phenomenology of human consciousness. For this reason, they are directly certifiable and are therefore undeniable and universal — they bind and govern the entire species called 'man'. Human beings differ from each other, individually and collectively, in their particular perceptions and theories regarding them; but, and this is the important point, the perceptions and theories are themselves eventually grounded in certain primordial, basic structures of our experience which, when scrutinized and articulated, become the central insights of *Jñāna-yoga* and their implications. I shall presently illustrate all this in the discussion to follow. Some implications are discussed as concepts and others as statements, depending upon whichever alternative is conducive to clear understanding.

Before proceeding further, let us note that all the concepts and propositions we shall discuss are implied by the three foundational insights of *Jñāna-yoga*, either individually or jointly. For this reason, they at all times stand as a perfectly coherent nexus, held together by phenomenological-analytical relations. Let it be reminded that logical relations come under analytical relations, and that the principal insights of *Jñāna-yoga* and their implications are *not* just logical, analytical truths; rather, as has already been made clear, they are *phenomenological-analytical* truths; that is, they arise from the very phenomenology of human experience; and when the experience is reflexively scrutinized and stated under the guiding eye of logic, one has statements of the insights. It is important to understand this point, in order that one may fully appreciate the claim that although the statements of the central insights of *Jñāna-yoga* and their implications are tautologies, and hence analytical, they are not empty of information; for they unmistakably point to structures of our experience. And just as even the allegedly empty tautologies of logic and mathematics are not uncoverable without hard and systematic work, so also the insights cannot be discovered without disciplined and systematic investigation of the phenomenology of human consciousness, conducted according to the highest standards of rational-experimental inquiry.

Perceiver-perceived distinction: Prior to the perceiver-perceived distinction, there is just perceiving, that is, there is neither the one nor the other. It is only through reflexive intelligence,[1] intelligence by which one can scrutinize one's own modes of being, sometimes also called 'reflexive consciousness' and 'reflexive awareness', that the single perceptual loop is cut, literally dissected, into the perceived on the one hand and the perceiver on the other. Ask yourself at your nearest opportunity, immediately after reading a page in a book, "when I was reading the page, was I aware of myself as the perceiver, the reader of the page, and of the page as the perceived?" The answer, as you will invariably discover, is certainly in the negative. There is just perceiving — reading, thinking, understanding, interpreting, and so on, but there was no awareness of yourself as the perceiver, the reader, or of the perceived, the page. What this means, then, is that it is only by rendering asunder the single perceptual loop that in a unitary manner contains and holds together the perceiver and the perceived that the perceiver-perceived distinction arises. The perceiver, as perceived by himself, through reflexive scrutiny, is the ego, also usually called the 'subject'. That which is perceived is the object, the object of consciousness, the object of cognition. The perceived may be a so-called physical object, a thought, an emotion, an image, an impluse, a dream, a hallucination, etc. The perceiver-perceived distinction is thus none other than the familiar subject-object distinction, and this distinction is the necessary condition for the possibility of any knowledge-enterprise. This is but another way of saying that the knower-known distinction is presupposed by every knowledge-inquiry, every epistemological investigation. If epistemology, the theory of knowledge, is the inquiry into our ways of knowing, how can it ever get started without acknowledging the knower-known distinction? And since the distinction, namely the knower-known distinction, is given directly and immediately, without the involvement of any of the senses or theories, and insofar as all epistemological inquires presuppose this distinction as self-given and self-evident, it is correct to say that all epistemological inquiries are transcendentally grounded. What precisely do I mean by 'transcendentally grounded'? Something is transcendentally grounded if it is wholly non-sensory; for is it not the case that if by 'phenomenon' we mean anything sensory, then to be transcendentally grounded is to be trans-phenomenal.

It is clear now that the certification of the perceiver-perceived distinction is through direct, phenomenological inquiry; that is, as soon as one begins to reflect upon experience, the experience is divided into the perceiver on the one hand and the perceived on the other — into the experiencer and the experienced. But, one might ask, where and in what manner has the distinction come to be made? It certainly could not have been drawn in and by the perceived; rather, it could only have been drawn in and by the perceiver — the perceiving consciousness, if you will. One might now be tempted to argue that were it not for the perceived there could be no perception at all. I submit that this objection misses the point at hand, for our question is *not* whether there could be perception without the perceived; rather, it is the question as to how and where, given there is perceiving, the perceiver-perceived distinction comes to be drawn. And I am saying that this distinction has its source in the perceiver and not in the perceived. That is, the perceiver-perceived distinction could only have been drawn in and by the perceiver. Has anyone observed something, say a tree, walking up to him and introducing itself as the perceived? Or when you were walking down the street, have you ever seen something, say a telephone-pole, placing a label upon itself to the effect, 'I am the perceived'? Nothing could be more preposterous and irrational than such a suggestion. On the contrary, it is the perceiver who, by reflecting on his own state of being, namely perceiving, declares the perceiver-perceived distinction. Hence the following proposition:

> The perceiver-perceived distinction has its source in the perceiver's ability to scrutinize his own states of being. Such an ability is called 'reflexive intelligence'. The perceiver-perceived distinction is drawn not in or by the perceived, the object, but in and by the perceiver, the subject.

The perceiver-perceived distinction is the primordial of all dualisms and is commonly known as the 'self-other distinction'.

> What is a phenomenon? A phenomenon is anything that is or can be an object of consciousness. That is, every object, actual or possible, of consciousness, no matter what it is, is a phenomenon, and every phenomenon is an actual or possible object of consciousness.

All our ordinary consciousness — ordinary states of consciousness — is relative consciousness, that is, consciousness of some object or other. Whatever it is that at any given time is an object of consciousness is called 'intentionality of consciousness' (simply, 'intentionality'). This is to say that all our ordinary states of consciousness are intentional. It now follows that *every intentionality, actual or possible, is a phenomenon and every phenomenon is an actual or possible intentionality.*

Western phenomenologists declare it as the central dictum of their phenomenology that *all* consciousness is intentional, meaning thereby that there can be no such consciousness as objectless consciousness. *Jñāna-yoga* challenges this claim. *Jñāna-yoga* does not regard this dictum as false; rather, it finds the claim limited and inadequate, in that it applies only to *ordinary* states of consciousness but not to all modes of consciousness; for, according to *Jñāna-yoga*, there is objectless consciousness, a topic which we shall discuss later. But let us ask now: how does the Western phenomenologist know that *all* consciousness is intentional? Has he investigated all states of consciousness, whatever 'all' means? No, he has conducted no such investigation; he merely examined ordinary states of consciousness, which include dreams and hallucinations, and concluded that all states of consciousness are intentional. No investigation is undertaken by which to clearly answer the question: are all states of consciousness intentional? It is interesting to note that when pressed the Western phenomenologist would answer by saying that the claim that all states of consciousness are intentional is true by *definition*. But the question is not whether it is a definitional truth, but rather whether there is a phenomenological — experiential — basis for the definition. If it has no experiential basis, the definition is arbitrary and therefore irrelevant to an inquiry into the phenomenology of human consciousness. Our point here, then, is that the Western phenomenologist's claim that all consciousness is intentional is not wholly false, for it correctly describes ordinary states of consciousness; its error consists of in the unexamined and dogmatic assertion that it applies to all states of consciousness, thereby definitionally excluding the possibility of objectless consciousness. Whether or not there is objectless consciousness is not a matter to be decided by easy definitional fiat but by rigorous experimental investigation. And insofar as understanding the very being of man and the world and gaining insight into reality is the chief goal of *Jñāna-yoga*, phenomenological investigation, under various names such as *Yoga*, is an integral component of the practice of *Jñāna-yoga*. In this manner, *Jñāna-yoga* has always been associated with the practice of psycho-physiological experimentation in one form or other of *Yoga*. It is only through such experimental inquiries, coupled with systematic analysis, that fundamental questions as the above can be answered.

Yes, all ordinary states of consciousness are undeniably intentional. But how can one claim on the basis of this fact alone that *all* consciousness is intentional? And if there is in fact some other basis for this claim, why does not the Western phenomenologist show just what it is? According to *Jñāna-yoga*, there is objectless consciousness, consciousness without an object; and there are clear-cut methods by which to experience and certify such a state of consciousness. To be sure, they are difficult methods and demand a great deal of intelligence and diligence on the part of the inquirer. But why should this be surprising? Does one become a fine mathematician or an accomplished physicist without intelligent, disciplined, hard work? Certainly not; if so, why does one think that the experimentation needed to settle questions concerning issues such as states of consciousness should be easy and effortless? It takes discerning intelligence, analytical acumen, patience, and effort for systematic investigation of the varieties of states of human consciousness, on which alone as basis can fundamental questions be answered. We shall later indicate some of the techniques of phenomenological investigation relevant to *Jñāna-yoga*. Suffice it for now to note the following:

> There is on the one hand a plurality of states of intentional consciousness — states of relative consciousness — and on the other there is but a single state of non-intentional, non-relative, objectless, transcendental consciousness.

We have said earlier that all objects, actual or possible, of consciousness — that is, all actual or possible intentionalities of consciousness — are phenomena. A moment's reflection reveals that some objects of consciousness are both in space and time, whereas others are only in time. Thus, for example, the so-called external objects are both in space and time, somewhere and somewhen; whereas thoughts, emotions, mental images, etc. are only in time and not in space, the kind of space in which the so-called external objects are said to be. But whether an object — an intentionality — is both in space and time or just in time, all objects are in time. Ans since every actual or possible object of consciousness is a phenomenon and every phenomenon is an actual or possible object of consciousness, we are entitled to declare the following proposition:

> All phenomena are in time. Therefore, it is time and not space that governs all phenomena, the entire world of phenomenal existence.

But, let us ask, what does it mean to say that all phenomena–intentionalities are in time? It means to say that all phenomena are subject to change; that is, change is the heartbeat of all phenomena; and this is precisely what is expressed by the

Principle of Dependent Origination: this arising, that arises; and this ceasing to be, that ceases to be. We may now define 'phenomenon' as follows: *To be a phenomenon is to arise and pass away.* The world of phenomena is thus through and through time-bound existence. Just pay attention to the endless stream of thoughts and emotions constantly arising and passing away, you will see the point. Another way of expressing this idea is to say that the world of phenomena is one of change and dynamism. *Time is but the form of this primordial dynamic that governs all phenomena.*

How does the sense of time arise? Answer: through the discernment of change, which is dynamism. Mountains arise and crumble, continents are formed and dissolved, stars are born and die away, seasons come and go, organisms are born, grow old, and die, and so on. In a word, worlds come into being and pass away. The entire nexus of intentional existence is thus time-bound. This is the same as saying that in the world of phenomena there can be nothing which has own-existence and own-nature. Hence the declaration: *no phenomenon has self-existence or self-nature. In a word, all phenomena are empty — devoid of own-nature and own-existence.* To say that every phenomenon arises and passes away in dependence upon other phenomena is to say that the existence and nature of all phenomena are relative and dependent. It now follows that 'dependent existence' and 'relative existence' mean the same as 'time-bound' existence. Phenomenal existence, then, is existence in the grip of time.

What is an absolute being? An absolute being is one which has own-existence and own-nature; consequently, such a being can be no part of the phenomenal world. The absolute and phenomena are mutually exclusive, for the reason that whereas no phenomena can have own-existence and own-nature, the absolute is that which has own-existence and own-nature. This is tantamount to saying that while phenomena are time-bound the absolute transcends time. Therefore, the following proposition:

Only phenomena can be actual or possible objects of consciousness — intentionalities; and the absolute, transcending time, cannot, in principle, be an object of consciousness.

We shall now show that the non-rational reality is indeed the absolute. Let us note first that reality is the *totality* of existence. And since there can, in principle, be nothing apart from the totality of existence, reality cannot be the effect of any cause; this in turn means that reality, unlike phenomena, does not arise and pass away. And since reality cannot be denied, reality is self-existent, the absolute. It can therefore be neither made to come into existence nor made to pass away. It simply is, has always been, and will ever be. Reality is spaceless and timeless; it is nowhere and nowhen, unlike phenomena, which are inevitably somewhere and somewhen. *Reality thus transcends the entire domain of phenomena.*

At this point, it will be instructive to briefly discuss the notion of reality as it occurs in Kant, a no mean practitioner of *Jñāna-yoga*, and compare and contrast it with that of reality in *Jñāna-yoga*. Let us start by clearly setting forth the Kantian meanings of 'phenomena' and 'noumena'. For Kant, 'phenomenon' means anything that is grasped through our senses and intellect; that is, anything that presents itself, through the instrumentality of the senses and mind, as an object of consciousness. More technically, phenomena are syntheses of manifolds of representations. And what is noumenon? Noumenon, according to Kant, is what a thing (phenomenon) is in itself, apart from our senses and intellect. Noumenon, in a word, is the thing-in-itself. It is to be noted that Kant talks of noumena,[2] the plural of noumenon. Thus, corresponding to, say, five phenomena, there are five noumena — five things-in-themselves. But the question to ask here is: Is Kant entitled to speak of noumena? The answer to this question leads us to one of the most profound implications of the central insights of *Jñāna-yoga*.

True, there is undeniably a variety and multiplicity of phenomena — existents. But how does it follow from this fact that there is also a variety and multiplicity of noumena? Phenomena are recognizable and numerically distinguishable by virtue of their different properties and spatio-temporal locations. Thus, I distinguish the book on the table from, say, the flower in the vase, as well as from an interesting thought I have had this morning about elementary particles. But does this fact, namely that one can so distinguish three objects — phenomena — entitle one to claim that there are three noumena, each corresponding to one of these three objects? If on Kant's own admission one does not and in principle cannot know what the book is in itself, what sense does it make to talk about three things-in-themselves? How is one justified in extending the concept of number and plurality, which is perfectly applicable to phenomena, to the noumenal which in principle and forever is unknowable by the senses and intellect? According to *Jñāna-yoga*, there are absolutely no grounds for speaking of the noumenal as a plurality. The noumenal is neither one nor many and is appropriately referred to as 'non-dual'. To think of the noumenal as plural is to commit the serious error of regarding the noumenal as phenomenal.

But, one might ask, what led Kant in the first place to speak of noume*na*? Is there something in his teaching that is the seed of this error? Yes, there is something profoundly wrong with Kant's extension of the concept of causality to the noumenal. Thus on the one hand Kant proclaimed that the category of causality, like the rest of his categories, is applicable only to phenomena; on the other hand, he nevertheless went on to regard the noumenon as the cause of the phenomenon. And since one does distinguish the so-called effects, one phenomenon from another, it is only natural that Kant thought that one noumenon — the cause of one phenomenon — can be distinguished from another — the cause of another phenomenon. This is one of the most serious errors in Kant's philosophy.

Jñāna-yoga is in full agreement with Kant in the latter's claim that the category of causality, like any other category, is applicable only to phenomena, and any attempt to extend the category beyond phenomena inevitably results in contradiction and absurdity. The concept of causality implies time-bound existence and therefore properly applies to phenomena, whose nature it is to arise and pass away. If so, to speak of the noumenon as the cause of the phenomenon is to think of the noumenon as also time-bound existence; but, according to Kant himself, the noumenon is in principle unknowable through the senses and intellect. In a word, the noumenon transcends space and time. Hence the contradiction. *Jñāna-yoga*, therefore, rejects as mistaken the application of the category of causality to the noumenal and therewith the notion of the noumenal as one of plurality. If no thing (phenomenon) can in principle be known to be what it is in itself, then it is surely unwarranted and irrational to talk about things-in-themselves (the so-called noumena).

What, then, is the relation between the noumenal and the phenomenal (the world of phenomena)? According to *Jñāna-yoga*, the relation is not a causal relation; rather, it is one of appearances under some superimpositional matrix; and we have seen earlier that different superimpositional matrices result in different worlds of phenomena. Thus *Jñāna-yoga's* explication of the nature of the relation between the noumenal and the phenomenal is based upon and flows from the Principle of Superimposition. This principle is the claim that the subject — the perceiver, the inquirer — in our case the human being, is not a passive register of some objective data, states of affairs; rather, what the inquirer perceives and how he conceives of it is inextricably bound up with his psycho-physiological constitution, that is, with his superimpositional apparatus, which includes his categorial framework. If this principle is true, then it follows that what there is manifests itself in different modes and manners to differently constituted subjects (of experience). This is to say that there is a reality, and differently constituted inquirers experience it differently and advance different descriptions of its manifestations. This is the main reason for *Jñāna-yoga's* rejection of all talk of noumena and for its assertion of a non-dual reality, whose various manifestations, as grasped and described by differently constituted inquirers, constitute the different worlds of phenomena. Put pointedly, if the Principle of Superimposition is true, then it is senseless to talk about a plurality of underlying (noumenal) realities; for, on one's own admission, these so-called noumena are for ever — in principle — beyond the ken of our senses and intellect. Why then preserve the absurd notion of the noumenal as one of plurality? It meets the highest standards of rational-experimental inquiry to regard the noumenal as non-dual rather than plural; and we have established earlier that the non-dual reality is transcendental — transcends space, time, the senses, and intellect. This non-dual reality cannot be demonstrated, for all demonstration is dual-dwelling between grounds and consequences, between premises and conclusions. If the non-dual is all that there is (or can ever be), what could serve as a demonstration of it? All demonstration takes place within this non-dual reality, there being nothing besides it by which to demonstrate the non-dual reality itself. This is but another way of saying that the non-dual reality cannot be demonstrated because all demonstration, all proof, all explanation presupposes dualism. One might ask now: why should one accept this thesis of non-dual reality if it cannot, on your own admission, be demonstrated? The answer is straightforward: what sense does it make to ask for a demonstration, after it has been shown (above) why the non-dual reality cannot be demonstrated? Is it any more sensible than asking for, say, 103.2 electrons, after it has been shown that the concept of a fractional electron is absurd and self-contradictory? Certainly not; such a question only goes to show that one has not understood the argument for the indemonstrability of the non-dual reality; or having understood it, one has rejected it for some reasons; and it will be interesting to examine such purported reasons. It is of signal importance to note that the concepts 'meaning', 'explanation', and 'proof' as well as 'demonstration' are all dualistic; that is, they become meaningless and empty as soon as dualism is denied; if so, what does it mean to demonstrate the being of the non-dual reality? These remarks apply equally to those various claims to show (and in some cases, to have shown) that reality is ultimately material, mental, etc. For have we not often enough heard the dinning chorus that reality is matter in motion, reality is mind — an idea — reality is spirit, without realizing the utter absurdity of such claims to demonstrate monism?[3] The simple truth is that monism cannot, in principle, be demonstrated, for all demonstration requires dualism. Monism, in its genuine indemonstrability, is formless, and hence nameless; and how can the formless be demonstrated? Every demonstration belongs in and pertains to the realm of forms, phenomena. Therefore, every claim to have demonstrated monism is wholly mistaken; for the monism it has allegedly demonstrated is not monism in the genuine, logical sense of the formless, but monism of some form or other, such as matter — elementary particles — mind, and so on. These failures only serve to illustrate the essential indemonstrability of monism in the formless sense, which is its only correct and logically impeccable sense. Needless to say, all other senses of monism are either errors or pretences; they are pseudo-monisms. For if monism is the thesis that all phenomena are manifestations of a single reality, which itself transcends phenomena, how can one rationally advance such claims as reality is physical (material), reality is mental, etc.? For is it not clear from the very claims themselves that they are self-contradictory and absurd? Let us take the view that reality is material. Matter is but one subset of phenomena, mind another, and so on; if so, is it not self-contradictory to claim to have established monism in the formless sense when the claim assigns a form — matter — to the one reality whose myriad manifesations are the worlds of phenomena? The inescapable conclusion, then, according to *Jñāna-yoga*, is that *monism, in the sense of the formless, cannot, in principle, be demonstrated*. It is of supreme importance to understand why the non-dual reality cannot be demonstrated. It is among the highest goals of *Jñāna-yoga* to comprehend in ever greater depth and clarity the indemonstrability of the non-dual reality.

The non-dual reality transcends all worlds of phenomena, all domains of demonstrability — that is, all realms of duality. It is precisely for this reason that no demonstration of the non-dual reality is possible. The Principle of Superimposition, which is the fruit of sustained reflection, including reflexion, and rigorous analysis of the phenomenology of human experience and knowledge, does not, and cannot, display or demonstrate the non-dual reality; rather, the principle calls our attention to

— awakens us to — the non-dual reality, whose varieties of manifestations are the worlds of phenomena. The principle's claim to truth is its irrefutability, which at once constitutes the indemonstrability of the non-dual reality.

How does the Principle of Superimposition awaken us to the non-dual reality? I shall now sketch the argument on behalf of the contention that the Principle of Superimposition does point to the non-dual reality. According to this principle, the nature of the experience and knowledge of a certain kind of beings is inseparably bound up with their psycho-physiological makeup. This means that what there is, is experienced and described differently by differently constituted beings. We ourselves bear witness to this claim by noting that changes in the physiology — biochemistry — of an organism bring about psychological changes, and therewith changes in experience and knowledge. Is it not rational, then, to hold that there is a reality and different kinds of beings experience and describe it differently? That reality is indeed the non-dual reality; it has to be non-dual reality, for, on our own admission, it transcends the senses and intellect, the superimpositional devices. Or, one might ask, is it rational to think that reality, like phenomena, is plural? We have argued that it is absurd and self-contradictory to talk of noume*n*a. In light of the above considearations, it is rational to subscribe to a non-dual reality, rather than to the unwarranted and self-contradictory thesis of reality as plural. In order to refute this conclusion, one needs to refute the Principle of Superimposition, and it cannot be refuted because every attempted refutation presupposes the principle, not as an obscure theoretical assumption but rather as a phenomenological-analytical truth. Thus every purported refutation of the Principle of Superimposition will be self-stultifying, since the proposed refutation cannot even begin without confirming that which it is to refute.

I come now to further considerations of the non-dual reality. We have shown, in connection with our discussion of the Principle of Dependent Origination, that all phenomena are devoid of own-being and own-nature. Insofar as every phenomenon arises and passes away in dependence upon other phenomena, no phenomenon can be said to exist on its own or have its own-nature. To say that every phenomenon lacks own-existence and own-nature is to say that every phenomenon is empty. Hence the declaration that all phenomena are empty of own-being and own-nature. The non-dual reality, in that it transcends space, time, the senses, and intellect, is also empty, that is, empty of phenomena. This is the meaning of the claim of *Jñāna-yoga* that reality is Void,Emptiness (*śūnyatā*). In what sense is the non-dual reality Void (Emptiness)? The non-dual reality is not constituted of any and all those things (phenomena) which are the products of the activity of superimposition. It is devoid of everything pertaining to the perceptual-conceptual realm. In other words, the non-dual reality is not a thing (an object, a phenomenon); nor is it nothing in the sense of utter absence and blankness; rather, it is no-thing. To be a thing is to be one among many particulars; and to be a particular is to have temporal location; and since reality transcends phenomena — particulars — it is non-spatial and non-temporal. Thus reality is not itself a thing; nor is it constituted of things. It is neither one nor many, since it transcends number and plurality. In a word, the non-dual reality is Void,Emptiness. This Emptiness is at once Fullness, the fullness of all existence in its inexhaustible variety and multiplicity. Not itself being a phenomenon, the Void, the non-dual reality, is formless and therefore also nameless. Yet it is the fount of all things, all phenomena — all forms and names. If reality is a thing, it will just be one among many things and not all things and therefore reality. Hence it is self-contradictory to think of reality as some*thing*, no matter how lofty and inspiring.

Just as the higher truth (*paramārtha*), itself not being one among several views, is fully compatible with all views, so also the non-dual reality, itself not being one among many phenomena, is in full harmony with all phenomena as well as all theories and views about phenomena. The non-dual reality simply is; it is neither one nor many; it is neither rational nor irrational; it is purely non-rational and therefore transcends the senses and intellect.

It should be clear by now that the Principle of Superimposition and that of Dependent Origination together point to — awaken us to — the non-dual reality as Void. The argument for this claim may succinctly be expressed as follows: every phenomenon is the result of superimpositions of percepts and concepts — forms and names — on the non-dual reality; and every phenomenon arises and passes away in dependence upon other phenomena. Thus all phenomena are time-bound, and since the non-dual reality transcends time, it is neither a phenomenon nor phenomena. That is, it is devoid of phenomena — things. This is just what was it is to say that the non-dual reality is Void, Emptiness.

For *Jñāna-yoga*, then, it is of paramount importance to realize the non-dual reality, the Void, Emptiness, jointly implied by the Principle of Superimposition and that of Dependent Origination. In realizing this, one realizes the indemonstrability of the non-dual reality. I shall now take up the question whether this is all that *Jñāna-yoga* has to say about the non-dual relity.

Having understood, through a systematic analysis of the phenomenology of human experience and knowledge, that there is a non-dual reality transcending the senses and intellect, *Jñāna-yoga* goes on to inquire whether this non-dual reality is for ever beyond human experience. Accoding to *Jñāna-yoga*, the non-dual reality is experienceable, but it is an experience in which all dualities are absent. I shall now set forth the reasoning behind this claim. Let us start by asking the question: what prevents us from experiencing the non-dual reality? Answer: our activity of superimposition — categorial activity. The non-dual reality manifests itself to us as different phenomena under different superimpositional networks. It now follows that in order to experience the non-dual reality, one should, as it were, shut off the machinery of superimposition; on switching off the superimpositional network, all manifestations, that is, all phenomena, disappear and vanish away. And on the disappearance of phenomena, there arises non-relative, non-intentional consciousness. This consciousness, unlike ordinary, intentional consciousness, is non-dual since it is not consciousness of any*thing*, of any phenomenon. The question now arises: how does one turn off the superimpositional machinery? It is at this point that *Jñāna-yoga* requires the inquirer to undertake careful study of the techniques of *Rāja-yoga*,[4] the *yoga* of psycho-physiological investigation. The purpose of such a study is to discover from among the variety of techniques of *Rāja-yoga* those that are best suited to oneself for bringing about the cessation of all superimpositional activity. If superimposition is what is responsible for our experience of phenomena, then it is only logical that on the removal of superimposition there will no longer be experience of phenomena but only of the non-dual reality. In fact, at the very beginning of his great work, *The Yoga-Sūtras*, Patañjali describes *Yoga* as "the inhibition — cessation — of the modifications of the mind" (*citta-vṛtti-nirodhaḥ*). It should now be clear that the modifications of the mind *are* the superimpositional activity. Thus it is the modifications of the mind that obstruct us from experiencing the non-dual reality.

We have already seen that all phenomena are in time; consequently, the elimination of the sense of time is necessary to transcend phenomena — time-bound existence. And, this is the important point, there will be apprehension of phenomena and therefore the sense of time as long as there are mental modifications. Therefore, the way to obliterate the sense of time is by bringing the mind to a standstill. It might be mentioned here that sensory-deprivation experiments, such as John Lilly's,[5] clearly show that even if all external stimuli are eliminated by keeping a person in equilibrium with his environment the person will have a sense of time, because there still are mental modifications — thoughts and emotions arising and passing away. The mental modifications, that is, the arising and passing away of thoughts and emotions, as a sequence of events constitute the subject's sense of time; and as long as there are the modifications of the mind, there will be the sense of time. Hence the cessation of mental modifications is necessary for the cessation of the sense of time. Thus it is the mind that holds the key for the dynamic of time and therewith to the world of phenomena. It is unmistakably clear now that the cessation of the sense of time is at once the cessation (disappearance) of phenomena; and when phenomena disappear, consciousness is no longer consciousness of objects; that is, it is no longer the ordinary, intentional consciousness. Another way of making this same point is to say that the cessation of mental modifications results in the breakdown of the ordinary, intentional structure of consciousness. With the collapse of intentional consciousness, there arises the state of objectless consciousness — non-intentional, non-relative consciousness. Someone might now feel provoked to ask: "Are you saying that this objectless consciousness is the non-dual reality? Why did you have to disguise so long this idealistic theory of reality? You could have quite some time ago made this point clear." I welcome these questions, for they give me the opportunity to clarify certain basic misunderstandings as well as lack of understanding concerning objectless consciousness. Accordingly, the bulk of the remaining part of this chapter will be devoted to answering these questions and establishing the thesis that the objectless consciousness is need the non-dual reality.

I shall start by noting that the term 'idealistic theory of reality' is positively misleading in the present context; for the various idealistic theories of reality one encounters in the history of philosophy, particularly in the West, claim that ultimate reality is of the nature of *mind*, a thesis quite different from that advanced by *Jñāna-yoga*, according to which ultimate reality is of the essence of *objectless consciousness*. Even a cursory examination of Western philosophy clearly shows that the thinkers in the West have rarely, if ever, distinguished between mind and consciousness;[6] consequently, it should not be surprising that the so-called idealistic philosophers of the West embrace and advance the view that ultimate reality is of the essence of mind. Even Descartes, who is usually regarded as having set up the unbridgeable gulf between mind and body, considered the former to be the same as the self (the "I"), as is clear from the following remarks: " . . . For it might indeed be that *if I entirely ceased to think, I should thereupon altogether cease to exist.*"[7] I am saying that it is precisely their failure to distinguish between mind and consciousness that has led the idealistic philosophers of the West to the claim that ultimate reality is mind — mental.

It is therefore misleading to construe the contention of *Jñāna-yoga* — that ultimate reality is of the essence of objectless consciousness — an an idealistic theory of reality.

Let us ask now: What are the objections against the view that mind and consciousness are one and the same? It is to be noted first that mind is a phenomenon, in that it is an *object* of consciousness. Let it be emphasized that one's theories as to how mind and body interact have no bearing on the fact that mind is a phenomenon, an object of consciousness, an intentionality. By 'mind' I mean nothing mysterious or transcendental; on the contrary, mind is no more and no less than mental activities; for this reason, mind is best construed as a field of energy; it is sheer dynamism, a nexus of activities and potential for activities — mental activities. To be aware of mind is to be aware of one's thoughts and the activity of thinking. Mind is not a container of thoughts; rather, thought and thinking *are* mind; mind is an energy field, the fluctuations in which are phenomenologically cognized as thinking and thoughts. It is worth emphasizing that it makes no difference to this point — that mind is a field of energy — whether one insists upon thought-talk or thinking-talk, as long as one acknowledges that thinking and thoughts belong to a clearly distinguishable mode of our being; and it is not in anyone's power to deny that we are immediately and clearly aware of two modes of our being, namely, the physical and the mental; thus does one distinguish between one's experience of a stone from one's experiences of a thought, an emotion, a mental image, etc. Nor is there any need to deny that there are certain neurophysiological processes as correlates of thinking and thoughts. The point of all these observations is that mind and consciousness are *not* one and the same. Mind is a phenomenon and is therefore time-bound; and, like all other phenomena, mind arises and passes away. Mind is an object of consciousness and cannot function without consciousness. Do we not speak of conscious and unconscious thoughts? Yes, but what do we mean by 'unconscious thoughts'? 'Unconscious thought' does not mean thought in a matrix devoid of consciousness; rather, it means thought of which the subject is not aware *as an object of consciousness* that is, thought which has not become an object of reflection. A great deal of our everyday activities are unconscious in this sense. Just think of your driving a car, you will be amazed at the variety of actions you perform without any deliberate thinking; and that is just what I mean by 'unconscious thought' and 'unconscious activity'. It is surely absurd to suggest that you were unconscious — bereft of consciousness — while driving the car. To take another example, suppose I ask you if you saw John Litehead this morning, and you say 'yes'. I then ask you, 'was he wearing a blue tie'? You will say either 'yes' or 'no' or 'I did not notice'. What do you mean when you say, 'I did not notice'? You obviously mean that although you saw John and spent considerable time with him this morning, the details of his dress did not become objects of you consciousness; that is, they did not become objects of your attention and reflection. This same point may be made by saying that something is an object of one's consciousness when one pays attention, and one is unconscious of something when one has not paid attention.

In this context, it is important to note that thinking is an activity — a process — that takes place in time; thoughts arise and pass away. This is the same as saying that thoughts are through and through time-bound. There is thus for thoughts a duration, no matter how small, the span between rising and passing away. In a word, thought takes time. All these considerations lend support to the thesis of *Jñāna-yoga* that mind is an energy field, the perturbations in which are thinking and thoughts.

The claim that mind and consciousness are not one and the same can further be substantiated by the following observations. One can think away everything but consciousness. But why is it that one cannot think away consciousness? Answer: thinking requires consciousness, and that is why consciousness cannot be thought away. Furthermore, if mind and consciousness were the same, then when mental modifications are brought to a cessation, consciousness, too, will be brought to a cessation. Such, however, is not the case, for, on stilling the mind, consciousness does not vanish away. And this fact clearly shows that mind and consciousness are not one and the same, and it is therefore a serious error to identify mind and consciousness. It is not consciousness but rather intentionalities — objects — of consciousness that vanish away with the cessation of mental modifications. Put another way, upon the cessation of mental modifications, the intentional structure, characteristic of our everyday, ordinary experience, breaks down; with such a breakdown, all objects — phenomena — disappear and there is just consciousness — consciousness without objects. And, according to *Jñāna-yoga*, such objectless consciousness is indeed the non-dual reality. One might now object, 'I understand that mind is a phenomenon and is not to be identified with consciousness, but I do not see any grounds for the claim that objectless consciousness is the non-dual reality.' In what follows, I shall clearly set forth arguments in defense of the claim that objectless consciousness *is* the non-dual reality.

Before proceeding further, it is in order first to clarify certain points about relative consciousness and objectless consciousness. What is relative consciousness? Relative consciousness is consciousness relative to some phenomenon — that is, intentional consciousness, consciousness of some object, some phenomenon or other. It has the polar structure (intentional structure) of consciousness *and* object of consciousness. Rigorously speaking, it is not consciousness that has the intenetional, polar structure; rather, it is the *experience* whose polar structure is of consciousness-versus-object of consciousness, the perceiver-versus-the perceived, the subject-versus-object. Thus consciousness itself is one pole of experience — ordinary, everyday experience — the object being the other. Consciousness itself does not have any structure. How so? Because to have a structure is to be an object, a phenomenon; and since consciousness can never, in principle, be an object, it follows that consciousness is structureless; if you are still unconvinced, try as you will to discover the structure of consciousness. I assure you that you will return wholly baffled, only to admit that consciousness cannot be captured as an object and hence it has no structure. Thus, consciousness, one pole of ordinary experience, is devoid of structure; on the other hand, the other pole, namely, intentionality, the object, is necessarily a structure. It is therefore a phenomenological-analytical truth that every phenomenon, actual or possible, has a structure and anything that has a structure is a phenomenon, actual or possible. The only way to refute this claim is to produce an object without a structure or produce some*thing*(!) with a structure but is not an object. You will quickly realize that such instances are self-contradictory, in light of the phenomenology of our experience.

It should be evident by now that it is not consciousness which is of a polar structure, but rather it is experience which is polar. One pole of experience is consciousness, which is devoid of structure; the other pole is the object, which necessarily has some structure. And since every object is a phenomenon, the polar structure of ordinary experience can also be expressed as one of consciousness-versus-phenomena. And since all phenomena are time-bound existence, one pole of our ordinary experience is always locatable in the world of phenomena. And since the other pole, namely consciousness, never appears as an object, as one among many phenomena, consciousness is not an object and therefore does not have any structure. In a word, consciousness is non-phenomenal. Expressed differently, consciousness transcends phenomena — space and time, the senses and intellect. At this point, it is important to caution the reader against seduction by such proclamations as, 'consciousness is a stream'. In fact, William James, the American psychologist and philosopher so proclaimed.[8] According to *Jñāna-yoga*, such a view is mistaken. Let us ask: what does one mean by the claim that consciousness is a stream? Surely one cannot mean that one experiences consciousness itself as a stream, whose distinguishing trait is dynamism. But what constitutes this stream? The answer, according to *Jñāna-yoga*, is that the ceaseless arising and passing away of phenomena — objects of consciousness — is the stream; and this is rightly so, because all phenomena are in time, and change and dynamism are time itself. Thus it is not consciousness that is a stream; rather, it is phenomena arising and passing away that constitute the stream. It is one of the most profound insights of *Jñāna-yoga* that consciousness is neither an object nor an agent. Consciousness does *not* do anything; it is merely there; in a word, it is presence itself, just being so. Once again, this is consistent with the thesis that consciousness transcends time, and since all activity — necessarily implying change — takes place in time, it is clear that to say that consciousness transcends time is to say that it transcends the entire domain of change, dynamism, and activity. This is just what it is to say that consciousness does not do anything. The reader is onece again urged to engage in experimentation and observation, in order to determine for himself the truth or falsity of the claim of *Jñāna-yoga* that consciousness is not a doer, not an agent. Claims such as these cannot be settled by clever definitions and dogmatic and uncritical assertions. The only way to determine their truth or falsity is rigorous rational-phenomenological inquiry, which includes the methods and procedures of *Rāja-yoga*. Nothing less will do. We conclude that the view that consciousness is a stream is false and mistaken.

We have shown above that our ordinary experience is constituted of two poles, consciousness and objects (phenomena). Thus it is not consciousness that has a polar structure but experience — ordinary experience. The question now arises: what is the difference between consciousness as a pole and objectless consciousness? According to *Jñāna-yoga*, there is no difference whatsoever between the two. That is, consciousness, *qua* consciousness, is the same whether as a pole or as objectless consciousness. Upon the disappearance of the object-pole of ordinary experience with the cessation of mental modifications, consciousness which hitherto was a pole becomes objectless consciousness. We may schematically express this idea as follows: Consciousness + objects = ordinary experience; it now follows that consciousness = ordinary experience – objects. And this is in perfect accord with the contention of *Jñāna-yoga* that objectless consciousness is attained by eliminating mental modifications. Thus one starts with ordinary experience — experience with a polar structure — and by the methods of *Rāja-yoga* brings about the cessation of mental modifications; and with the cessation of mental modifications, the object-pole of ordinary experience vanishes away, leaving objectless consciousness as the residuum.

This in turn means that, upon the cessation of mental modifications, ordinary, polar experience itself becomes transformed into non-ordinary, non-polar experience; in a word, the polar structure of ordinary experience breaks down. This is the same as saying that non-polar experience *is* objectless consciousness.

I shall now proceed to show that the non-dual reality and objectless consciousness are identical — one and the same — by showing that anything that can correctly be affirmed or denied of the one can also be affirmed or denied of the other.

Let us note first that nothing can be positively said of the non-dual reality. The same is true of objectless consciousness. No image of either can be formed; neither can ever be experienced as an object, for all objects arise with mental modifications. In other words, mental modifications are necessary condition for the possibility of experience of objects. Consciousness, insofar as it cannot, in principle, be experienced as an object, is non-spatial, non-temporal, and transcends the senses and intellect. Similar is the case with regard to the non-dual reality. We have shown in our discussion of the Principle of Superimposition and that of Dependent Origination that the non-dual reality is experienced on the cessation of all superimpositional activity, which is but mental modifications. Thus one and the same condition is necessary for the possibility of experience of objectless consciousness as well as of the non-dual reality. Furthermore, just as consciousness is not a doer, so also the non-dual reality, transcending space, time, the senses and intellect, is not a doer. Consciousness and the non-dual reality are simply there; neither does anything, for all doing is activity; and since neither consciousness nor the non-dual reality is in time, it is simply absurd and self-contradictory to attribute any activity to them.

It is to be emphasized that no picture or image of consciousness or the non-dual reality can be formed. How so? Because it is only of objects (phenomena) one can form pictures and images; and since neither consciousness nor the non-dual reality is an object, a particular, a phenomenon, no pictures or images of either can be formed. If you are not convinced of the truth of this claim, try as you may to picture or image them, and you will certify that neither consciousness nor the non-dual reality is picturable. If consciousness and the non-dual reality are neither picturable nor visualizable in any other fashion, then surely it is absurd to suggest that consciousness is a stream, which certainly is picturable and therefore visualizable. Try sometime as an exercise in phenomenological investigation, akin to an exercise in *Rāja-yoga*, to picture and visualize consciousness and the non-dual reality. You will unfailingly discover that they simply cannot be pictured, imaged, or visualized. Thus both consciousness and the non-dual reality are beyond the powers of the senses and intellect; that is, both consciousness and the non-dual reality elude the senses and the mind. Paradoxically enough, though the mind talks *about* them, namely, consciousness and the non-dual reality, it is wholly impotent to image them, describe them, or *deny* them. For how can anyone consistently declare, "I am not conscious"? And how is it possible for anyone to be able to claim, "There is no reality"? The first claim is absurd and false in an obvious manner; and the second is just as absurd and self-contradictory as the first, in that how can anyone deny reality while one's own being is irrefragable testimony to the reality being denied?

We have shown earlier that the non-dual reality is *śūnyatā* — Emptiness — in the sense that it is devoid of any things (phenomena). The non-dual reality is therefore neither a phenomenon nor constituted of pehnomena. In brief, the non-dual reality is no-thing; it is no-thingness. It is precisely for this reason that the non-dual reality cannot be captured by the senses and the mind. The same is true of consciousness. It is also Emptiness and no-thingness. That consciousness is Emptiness — Void — and no-thingness is certifiable only through phenomenological inquiry; that is, one should experiment in order to determine the truth of the claim that consciousness, like the non-dual reality, is Emptiness. Just try to capture consciousness, and you will immediately see it is Emptiness. This means that there is absolutely no way by which to get a handle on consciousness. Put differently, it is only upon things that one can get a handle; and that consciousness cannot be got a hold upon goes to show that consciousness is not a thing — that consciousness is no-thingness.

Furthermore, consciousness, like the non-dual reality, has neither a beginning nor an end. The reason for this is that only time-bound existents — objects, things, particulars, in a word, phenomena — can have beginnings and ends. And since consciousness, like the non-dual reality, transcends time, it is absurd to talk about the arising and passing away of consciousness.

Consciousness, like ultimate reality, is non-dual, in that it is partless and non-composite. This is to say that consciousness is not made up of any parts or components. Consciousness is indivisible, and only things are divisible. And since the concept of whole implies parts, consciousness is not to be thought of as a whole either. Consciousness is thus neither a part nor a whole; in contrast, every phenomenon, without exception, is part of a whole and a whole made up of parts. We therefore conclude that consciousness and the non-dual reality are neither parts nor wholes. This should not be surprising, for how is it possible for Emptiness (Void) to be a part or a whole?

Consciousness, like the non-dual reality, is formless; for only things, objects (phenomena) can have some form or other; and, being formless, consciousness is also nameless. For is it not true that it is by form that we set one thing apart from another and label them by different names? Now someone might protest by saying, "this claim that consciousness is nameless is self-contradictory, for have you not yourself used the name 'consciousness'?" My answer is as follows: yes, I have used the term 'consciousness'. But does it mean that consciousness has a form, on discerning which it is set apart as one *thing* from another? We understand the term 'consciousness' not because we beheld the form of consciousness but because it is our very being, namely, presence itself. Thus 'consciousness' is *not* a name in the sense of the name of an object: rather, it is merely a device for the purpose of inquiry and discourse. But if one persists in the objection, I can only request for a description of the form of consciousness. I assure the reader that, no matter how hard he may try, he will discover no form of consciousness. Hence we conclude that consciousness is itself formless, although it is the basis for the experience of any form. A word of explanation is in order here, for one might mistakenly believe that it is mind and not consciousness that is the basis for the experience of forms. Such a belief is dispelled by noting that mind cannot function without consciousness. It is true, as has been shown, that forms arise with mental modifications; however, mental modifications and therewith forms cannot be detected — cannot be what they are — without consciousness. This is but another way of saying that although there can be consciousness without mental modifications, there can be no mental modifications and hence forms without consciousness. One of the simplest exercises by which to determine the truth of the claim that there is consciousness without mental modifications is as follows: sit quietly and command your mind to speak, saying that you will listen intently. You will discover that there is a brief span of time following the command during which there are neither sensations nor feelings nor thoughts — in a word, the mind becomes paralyzed. On experimenting with this exercise, you will certify that there is consciousness even where there are no mental modifications. It is to be noted, however, that because of the essential dynamism of mind such a state is of extremely short duration. One may also ask other people to do this exercise and tell what happens. The usual reply is, "there was *nothing*".

Another exercise which points to this same conclusion is the following. Look at any object in your visual field and close your eyes and observe what happens. One would say that an afterimage is formed. Yes, an afterimage is formed. But the question is: what is the state between the instant you closed your eyes and the instant the afterimage is formed? The answer is that there were neither sensations nor feelings nor thoughts. That is, there is just consciousness without any mental modifications.

It should be clear from all the foregoing considerations that anything that can be affirmed or denied of the non-dual reality can also be affirmed or denied of consciousness; that is, consciousness and the non-dual reality are identical, one and the same. It is of paramount importance to realize that consciousness and the non-dual reality are not two numerically distinguishable realities which happen to be identical; rather, they are one and the same reality, which is through and through non-dual.

The claim that consciousness and the non-dual reality are one and the same follows from the fact that one and the same condition is necessary for the experience of objectless consciousness and the non-dual reality, and the condition is the cessation of mental modifications. On switching off the superimpositional equipment, all phenomena disappear and there arises the experience of the non-dual reality. Upon the cessation of mental modifications, all objects disappear and there arises the experience of objectless consciousness. And since superimpositional activity *is* mental modifications and phenomena *are* objects, it follows that the non-dual reality *is* indeed objectless consciousness and *vice versa*.

I shall now consider what seems to be the most serious objection against the claim of *Jñāna-yoga* that ultimate reality is of the essence of consciousness. The objection runs as follows: "In your discussion of the Principles of Superimposition, Dependent Origination, and Two Truths, you yourself established that every claim to describe ultimate reality — the non-dual reality — is necessarily self-contradictory and absurd. If so, how can you now claim that ultimate reality is of the essence of consciousness?" Let me immediately acknowledge that this objection is understandable and deserves a clear and complete answer. My reply to the objection is follows.

Yes, it is quite true that every claim to *describe* ultimate reality is necessarily self-contradictory and hence false. But it is important to ask whether the claim of *Jñāna-yoga* that ultimate reality is of the essence of consciousness is a *description* of ultimate reality. A description, properly speaking, is a statement which attributes some property (or properties) to something, some entity. Here are a few examples of descriptive statements "This flower is red", "$\sqrt{2}$ is irrational", and "Protons are positively charged particles". It is to be at once noted that the claim of *Jñāna-yoga* is not "ultimate reality is conscious", but rather "ultimate reality *is* consciousness". What this means, then, is that the thesis of *Jñāna-yoga* is not a subject-predicate (thing-property) claim, but rather one of identity, namely, ultimate reality and consciousness are identical, one and the same. Several philosophers and religious thinkers have advanced claims about ultimate reality; some of these claims are as follows: ultimate reality is spirit, ultimate reality is person, ultimate reality is mind, and ultimate reality is matter. The important point here is that all these claims are descriptive, for one can always ask: What is spirit? What is person? What is mind? and What is matter? In keen contrast, the claim of *Jñāna-yoga* that ultimate reality is consciousness is an identity claim; for if someone were to ask, "what is consciousness?" no descriptive statement could be offered as a reply. How so? Because nothing can be said about consciousness, except that it is presence itself. There are no properties that can be attributed to consciousness. Why is it so? Because consciousness is not an object — a phenomenon — and only objects can be said to have properties. Let us emphasize that the statement "consciousness is presence" is not a subject-predicate claim; rather, it is an identity claim, namely, consciousness *is* presence (as contrasted with the statement, "consciousness possesses the property of presence)." What all this means is that consciousness, being formless, is not an object; and not being an object, it can have no properties. It is therefore clear that the thesis of *Jñāna-yoga* that ultimate reality is of the essence of consciousness is *not* a description of ultimate reality; rather, the thesis is the assertion that ultimate reality and consciousness are identical, one and the same. Put pointedly, ultimate reality is not something which possesses the property of being conscious but consciousness itself.

One might now say, "even so, the claim of *Jñāna-yoga* is a claim concerning ultimate reality; consequently, it cannot be exempt from self-contradiction and absurdity". In oder to answer this objection, let us briefly review some of the points we have made earlier. We have shown that ultimate reality (the non-dual reality) is *śūnyatā*, Emptiness, Void; we have also established that every claim to *describe* ultimate reality is necessarily self-contradictory and hence false. We have further shown that the higher truth — *paramārtha* — is non-perceptual and non-conceptual; in other words, the higher truth transcends the senses and intellect, and therefore transcends all categorial frameworks and and all categorial knowledge, actual and possible. For this reason, the higher truth, unlike lower truths — *saṁvṛtti* — cannot, in principle, be expressed in thought and language, but can only be experienced in direct, immediate intuition (*prajñā*) arising upon the cessation of all mental modifications. It is of the utmost importance to note here that in such intuition, unlike in the knowledge of lower truths, truth and being are inseparable and indistinguishable; that is, in every state of lower knowledge truth and being are separable and distinguishable, and this is as it should be, for the whole domain of lower truths is the domain of intentional consciousness — consciousness with objects; and with the cessation of mental modifications, the intentional structure of ordinary experience, that is, of the state of knowledge of lower truths, collapses, and this in turn means that truth and being are no longer separable and distinguishable, nay, they are one and the same; in a word, they are identical. Such a state of knowledge of the higher truth — *paramārtha* — is indeed *prajñā,* direct and immediate intuition. We have also shown that ultimate reality, like the higher truth, transcends the senses and intellect, and therefore can only be experienced on bringing about the cessation of superimpositional activity, which is but mental modifications. It is clear now that ultimate reality and the higher truth are one and the same; therefore, to experience the higher truth is to experience ultimate reality, and *vice versa.* We have further demonstrated that ultimate reality is *śūnyatā,* Emptiness, Void.

The question now arises: Must one accept the claim that ultimate reality is Void purely on the basis of intellectual inquiry or is there a way by which to certify what is intellectually established? The answer, according to *Jñāna-yoga,* is that no one should accept any claim unless it is open to experimental certification, and the claims of *Jñāna-yoga* are no exception. Thus we come to ask: What is one to do in order to determine the truth or falsity of the thesis of *Jñāna-yoga* that ultimate reality is *śūnyatā* (Void)? The answer by now should be obvious: Eliminate superimpositional activity; that is, bring mental modifications to a cessation. What is the residuum? By 'residuum' here I mean 'ultimate residuum', in the sense of that which remains because it cannot, in principle, be eliminated, made to disappear. According to *Jñāna-yoga*, the ultimate residuum *is* ultimate reality. The rationale for this claim is as follows: Only phenomena — objects — can be brought about or made to disappear; for all phenomena are time-bound existence; that is, phenomena arise and pass away. And since ultimate reality transcends time, it cannot, unlike phenomena, be made to appear and disappear; that which has an end has also a beginning, and *vice versa*; and since ultimate reality has no end, it has no beginning either. And it is precisely for this reason that ultimate reality cannot be eliminated, and hence it is the ultimate residuum. This ultimate residuum is also pure consciousness, consciousness without objects, pure awareness, *tathatā* (suchness, thusness); in a word, it is the Void (*śūnyatā*). It is thus clear that the intellectually apprehended truth that ultimate reality is non-dual and Void is existentially realized as objectless consciousness. And it is just this truth that is proclaimed by the thesis of *Jñāna-yoga* that ultimate reality is of the essence of objectless consciousness. In brief, ultimate reality and consciousness are identical. We therefore conclude that the claim of *Jñāna-yoga* that ultimate reality is of the essence of consciousness is certainly a claim pertaining to ultimate reality, but equally certainly it is not a *description* of ultimate reality. Rather, it is an identity claim, namely ultimate reality and consciousness are one and the same. 'Objectless consciousness' and 'ultimate reality' are thus two different terms for the same non-dual reality. Seen from the standpoint of the analysis of categorial knowledge, the claim is that when superimpositional activity is suspended the residuum is the non-dual reality — ultimate reality; and when the claim is put to test by actually suspending superimpositional activity, this non-dual reality is experienced as objectless consciousness. Upon the suspension of superimposition — mental modifications — the polar structure of ordinary, intentional experience collapses; that is, the object-pole of ordinary experience vanishes away, resulting in one's being as pure, objectless consciousness. It is worth noting here that for the person who actually attains the state of objectless consciousness there is no polar experience. Others — outsiders — may say that the person is in a state of experience of ultimate reality, but for the person himself his very being as objectless experience is ultimate reality. This is indeed the Void, the thusness and suchness. Thus the claim of *Jñāna-yoga* that ultimate reality is of the essence of objectless consciousness is a claim whose truth consists of the certification of the claim itself; the very process of certifying the claim constitutes its truth. Here truth is not certified by indirect, mediate ways of thinking, talking, and experimenting with things other than oneself; rahter, truth here is no more and no less than one's direct and immediate being as objectless consciousness. Note carefully how radical is the difference between the way of certifying the claim of *Jñāna-yoga* that ultimate reality and objectless consciousness are identical, and those of certifying categorial claims. For one thing, categorial claims are certified through the activity of superimposition — through the instrumentality of the senses and intellect; in striking contrast, the thesis of *Jñāna-yoga* can only by certified through the suspension of all superimpositional activity. And just for this reason, there is the corresponsding difference between the two kinds of experience: one is ordinary, intentional experience, that is, experience with a polar structure (consciousness-versus-objects); and the other is non-polar experience, that is, there is only consciousness but no objects. This is to be expected since objectless consciousness arises with the breakdown of the polar structure of ordinary experience; and the breakdown of the polar structure of ordinary experience itself is due to the cessation of all superimpositional activity, which is but mental modifications. What all this means, then, is that the thesis of *Jñāna-yoga* is not a lower truth (*saṁvṛtti*) rather, it is the higher truth itself (*paramārtha*) transcending all categorial frameworks. Thus the higher truth is inseparable from one's being. This is to say that ultimate reality, the higher truth, is the ultimate residuum, which is none other than objectless consciousness. The objectless consciousness, which is wholly non-contingent, is at once one's true being and ultimate, non-dual reality.

The inescapable conclusion flowing from the above arguments and analyses is that the claim of *Jñāna-yoga* that ultimate reality is of the essence of pure, objectless consciousness is neither a descriptive statement not self-contradictory; for if it were, it would be false. Quite the contrary, it is certifiable as true by any inquirer who can bring about the cessation of superimpositional activity. And this is the only way to certify its truth. This in turn means that the inquirer should undertake experimental-phenomeonological investigation of the calibre of *Rāja-yoga*, in addition to logico-analytical investigation. The higher truth is first to be intellectually comprehended; on such a comprehension, one conducts disciplined phenomenological inquiry in order to directly certify that which has been intellectually grasped. In this manner, *Rāja-yoga* (or any equivalent thereof) is an integral component of the practice of *Jñāna-yoga*. Mere head-spinning and tongue-twisting are not enough. There comes a point when all honest and serious inquirers should test their own reasoned claims about man, the world, and ultimate reality; and that is where experimental inquiry is absolutely indispensable. The claim of *Jñāna-yoga* is a claim of the higher truth and consequently cannot be vindicated by any means unequal to the claim itself.

In the remainder of this chapter, I shall raise and answer certain questions which, I am sure, will have occurred to the discerning reader. The answers are to be found in our treatment of the three central principles of *Jñāna-yoga*; nevertheless, I shall, for the sake of clarity, explicitly state them. The questions concern the status of the world of phenomena, God, and man.

1. What is the status of the world of phenomena? We shall begin by clearly setting forth the definitions of relevant concepts. In what follows, the terms 'reality' and 'ultimate reality' are used synonymously. 'Reality': that which exists without depending for its existence on anything other than itself. It is to be emphasized that this definition is *not* arbitrary; for if ultimate reality is that besides which nothing exists, then surely it will be self-contradictory to think of ultimate reality as existing by depending for its existence on something other than itself. If

someone objects to the above definition, it is incumbent upon him to produce an alternative definition of 'ultimate reality' which is neither arbitrary nor self-contradictory. It is the contention of *Jñāna-yoga* that every other definition (conception) of 'ultimate reality' is necessarily arbitrary and self-contradictory. This point will become clearer in the sequel.

'Unreality': that which cannot, in principle, exist; that is, unreality is that whose corresponding concept is self-contradictory and hence cannot, in principle, be exemplified. Here are some examples of unreality: married bachelor, the son of a barren woman, and square-circle. It is clear that unreality is that which cannot, in principle, be an object of our experience, actual or possible.

'Sublation': the activity of rectifying errors of judgment concerning fact or value. Thus a thirsty traveler in a desert thinks that he perceives water at a distance and rushes to the place only to find no water. He then concludes that his earlier perception is the perception of a mirage. That is, the judgment that there is water at a certain place is sublated (replaced), in light of new experience, by the judgment that it was a mirage. To take another example, in the everyday context we regard many objects, for instance the writing-desk, as solid; however, this judgment is sublated by that of modern physics that these objects are colonies of electrical charges in incessant motion. Now to an example of the sublation of value-judgments. At a certain time in his life, a man thinks that it will be good for him to get married and beget children; however, at a later time he prefers remaining a bachelor. Thus he has sublated his earlier judgment as to what is good for him by a later one.

The question now arises: what is the relation of the concepts of reality and unreality to that of sublation? It should immediately be clear that reality cannot, in principle, be sublated. Reason? Because sublation requires (presupposes) at least three things: the agent who does the sublating, the judgment to be sublated, and the sublating judgment. In other words, sublation is possible only in a domain of plurality, and since there can be nothing besides ultimate reality, ultimate reality cannot be sublated.

From what has been said thus far, it is evident that one phenomenon is sublatable by another and all phenomena are sublatable by ultimate reality, which itself is unsublatable. Sublatability, then, is the distinguishing trait of phenomena.

What, then, of unreality? Is it sublatable? According to *Jñāna-yoga*, unreality is neither sublatable nor non-sublatable. This claim, I am sure, will strike many as absurd and senseless, but that is only because they naively accept the law of excluded middle, which in the present context means the following: given anything whatever, either it is sublatable or it is not sublatable. Why is this view naive and simplistic? Because it is based on ignorance of the very notion of sublation. Let us clarify this matter. According to *Jñāna-yoga*, unreality is neither sublatable nor non-sublatable. The reasoning behind this claim is as follows: It will be a mistake to think that unreality is sublatable, because if unreality is that which cannot, in principle, be an object of our experience, actual or possible, how can it be sublated? Only something which can, in principle, be an object of our experience, actual or possible, can be sublated. Put differently, to think that unreality is sublatable is to commit the error of regarding unreality as a phenomenon, which undoubtedly is an object of our experience, actual or possible. And it will be equally erroneous to claim that unreality is non-sublatable, for only reality is non-sublatable since there can be nothing else than reality by which to sublate reality. This is to say that to think that unreality is non-sublatable is to mistakenly identify unreality with reality — a glaring contradiction. Thus, according to *Jñāna-yoga*, unreality is neither sublatable nor non-sublatable.

Let us ask now: What is the status of phenomena? It is to be first noted that phenomena are appearances of reality under superimposition (*adhyāsa*). From the standpoint of the concept of sublatability, phenomena, unlike unreality, are sublatable; this means that phenomena are *not* unreality. On the other hand, phenomena, unlike reality, are sublatable; hence, phenomena are *not* reality. Thus phenomena are neither real nor unreal. What does this mean? It means that it will be an error to think that phenomena are real, for if they were, they could not, contrary to fact, be sublated; and it will also be an error to think that phenomena are unreal, for, unlike unreality, phenomena are objects of our experience, actual or possible. It is for these reasons that *Jñāna-yoga* declares that phenomena are neither real nor unreal. Phenomena cannot be real, because every phenomenon depends for its existence on other phenomena — the Principle of Dependent Origination — and only reality exists without depending for its existence upon anything other than itself. Nor are phenomena unreal, for, unlike unreality, phenomena are objects of our experience, actual or possible. In short, phenomena are neither real nor unreal.

But what does it mean to say that phenomena are neither real nor unreal? It means, according to *Jñāna-yoga*, phenomena are dream-like and are essentially illusory. By this is meant that phenomena have an intermediate status — a status between that of reality and unreality. As has already been made clear, phenomena, unlike unreality, are actual or possible objects of our experience; on the other hand, phenomena, unlike reality, are not self-existent, and this is precisely what is meant by the declaration of *Jñāna-yoga* that phenomena have an intermediate status. Consider dreams; dreams are not unreal, for, if they were, how could they be objects of our experience? And, as certainly, dreams are not reality, for, if they were, they could not, contrary to fact, be sublated (by waking experience). To take another example, consider mirages. It is manifestly absurd to suggest that mirages are unreal, for, we actually experience them. It is worth emphasizing mirages are objective, in that everyone experiences them under certain circumstances. That is, mirages occur when certain objective conditions are fulfilled. If mirages are unreal, no one can experience them, and no objective truths about them can be arrived at. In other words, if mirages were unreal, there could be no physics of them. To say that mirages are illusory does not mean that they occur arbitrarily and capriciously; quite the contrary, they arise only when certain objective conditions are met. Has anyone experienced a mirage in a closet? And this is just what *Jñāna-yoga* means when it proclaims that the world of phenomena, being neither real nor unreal, is illusory. In a word, phenomena are appearances (of reality under superimposition).

The illusory but unreal nature of the world phenomena cannot be clarified better than through a classic illustration due to Śankara, namely, the rope-snake illustration, which is as follows. Suppose a man walks into the barn in the middle of the night to check the fodder for his cattle, steps on something, and shouts in fear and panic that he has stepped on a snake. It is to be noted that the person displays various signs of being frightened, such as racing heart, profuse sweating, froth at the mouth, etc. Now, another person, on hearing the cry of fear, rushes into the barn with a lamp, and discovers that the man has actually stepped on a rope and not a snake. The question now is: What exactly is the status of the snake the first person thought he stepped on? According to *Jñāna-yoga*, the snake is neither real nor unreal. The snake is not real, for, if it were, it could not have been sublated by the rope; nor is the snake unreal, for, it if were, it could not have been in the first place an object of one's experience. What this means, then, is that the snake is an appearance — a phenomenon — and the distinguishing feature of all phenomena is sublatability. The snake is the product of the activity of superimposition on the part of the person; he has mistakenly attributed the properties of snake to what he stepped on. But when the lamp is brought, the snake has disappered and instead there is only the rope. It is extremely important to note that the snake-experience would not have been possible had there been no rope in the barn. The rope is the reality which, under superimposition, appears as a snake. Just so, there is reality, which, under different superimpositional frameworks, appears as the variety of worlds of phenomena; and just as the snake has disappeared when the lamp is brought, so also when the superimpositional activity is brought to a cessation, the world of phenomena disappears and one experiences the ultimate, non-dual reality. And we have shown that the non-dual reality is none other than pure — objectless — consciousness.

It is easy to understand now why *Jñāna-yoga* regards the world of phenomena as magical, illusionary, and lacking own-existence and own-nature. This does not, however, mean that phenomena are unreal. Is it not magical that what was thought to be a snake at one moment appears as a rope in the next? This thesis that the world of phenomena is magical, illusionary, and non-self-existent is expressed through the concept of *māyā*, a profound concept of *Jñāna-yoga*. Yet no other concept of *Jñāna-yoga* is more misunderstood and misinterpreted than that of *māyā*. For this reason, we will do well to clarify this concept in some detail.

The concept of *māyā* is often understood by many as connoting unreality. But in light of our explication of the concepts of reality, unreality, and sublation, it is a grave error to think that *Jñāna-yoga* teaches that the world of phenomena is unreal; on the contrary, according to *Jñāna-yoga*, the world of phenomena is one of appearances, and not unreality. The concept of *māyā* can be explicated from three standpoints, in none of which it implies that the world of phenomena is unreal. Here are the three senses of *māyā*: (1) Psychologically speaking *māyā* is our persistent tendency to regard appearances as reality and *vice versa*. In terms of the criterion of sublatability, *māyā* is our constant propensity to regard the sublatable as the unsublatable and *vice versa*. (2) From an epistemological point of view, *māyā* is our ignorance (*avidyā*) as to the difference between appearances and reality. Reality is that which cannot in principle be sublated by any other experience, whereas appearances (phenomena) are those which in principle can be sublated by other experiences. Sublation is possible, as we have already demonstrated, only where distinctions exist, and since reality transcends all distinctions, the experience of reality cannot be sublated. On the other hand, the realm of appearances is necessarily one of distinctions and plurality and is therefore sublatable. This is tantamount to saying that one appearance can be sublated by another and all appearances can be sublated by reality. It is only by being unaware of this distinction between the sublatable and the unsublatable that one mistakenly believes that appearances are reality. In other words, ignorance as to the nature of reality is the foundation of *māyā*. It is clear, then, that only the unsublatable, the undifferentiated, is the non-dual is reality. The changing world of our senses, emotions, and intellect is an appearance. According to *Jñāna-yoga*, *māyā* is beginningless and endless, unthinkable, and inexpressible. *Māyā* is unthinkable, because all thinking has its origin in it; *māyā* is inexpressible, because language has its basis in it. *Māyā* is thus the warp and woof of the world of appearances — the world of the senses, emotions, and intellect. (3) From an ontological point of view, *māyā* is the creative power of reality by virtue of which the world of variety and multiplicity comes into existence.

Thus to say that the phenomenal world is *māyā* in the sense of illusion is not to say that the phenomenal world is unreal but rather an appearance, which has its foundation in reality. We have already established that appearances, unlike unreality, are sublatable. For this reason, there can be no such thing as pure illusion; on the contrary, every illusion is grounded in reality. In other words, illusions — which are certainly appearances — unlike unreality, are genuine components of our experience. Our answer, then, to the question concerning the status of the world of phenomena is as follows: the phenomenal world, like illusions, is not an independent (self-existent) reality but is grounded through and through in the sole ultimate, non-dual reality.

2. What, according to *Jñāna-yoga*, is the status of God? Consistent with its distinction between appearance and reality, *Jñāna-yoga* distinguishes two conceptions of God: God with qualities and relations and God without qualities and relations, respectively known as *Saguṇa-Brahman* (also called *Īśvara*) and *Nirguṇa-Brahman*. It should be obvious that the former conception belongs to the lower, conventional, mundane, relative, practical standpoint, and the latter to the higher, unconditioned, supramundane, absolute standpoint. *Saguṇa-Brahman* is God thought of as the cause, creator, sustainer, and destroyer of the universe. It is *Saguṇa-Brahman* that men worship under different names and forms, such as Jaweh, Allāh, Jesus, Rāma, Kṛṣṇa, Śiva, and a myriad others. It is God as *Saguṇa-Brahman* that is endowed with such qualities as love, kindness, mercy, and justice. *Saguṇa-Brahman* is God who stands in relation to man and the world. In brief, *Saguṇa-Brahman* is personal God. But

since qualities and relations can only belong in the realm of appearances (phenomena), *Saguṇa-Brahman* is God as appearance and not reality. On the other hand, *Nirguṇa-Brahman*, being reality beyond names and forms, is neither the cause nor the creator nor the sustainer nor the destroyer of the universe. God as *Nirguṇa-Brahman* can neither be worshipped nor prayed to. God as *Nirguṇa-Brahman* is ultimate, non-dual reality, which is but pure, objectless consciousness.

How profound is the distinction of *Jñāna-yoga* between *Saguṇa-Brahman* and *Nirguṇa-Brahman* — between lower truths and the higher truth — can be realized through even so much as a glance at the religious history of mankind. There is no need to emphasize that the religious history of man is fraught with zealotry, fanaticism, conflict, cruelty, bloodshed, and countless horrors and wars, all of which are committed in the name of God. How do we account for this strange, bizarre, and tragic saga? The answer, according to *Jñāna-yoga*, is clear and straightforward. Each group of human beings, being wholly oblivious to the distinction between *Saguṇa-Brahman* and *Nirguṇa-Brahman* — lower truth and the higher truth — advances absolute claims on behalf of its own *Saguṇa-Brahman*, and in this manner one *Saguṇa-Brahman* is pitted against another as ultimate reality; and since each group is as firmly convinced as the other of the truth of its own religion and single-mindedly committed to defending its own conception of *Saguṇa-Brahman*, conflict and opposition are inevitable. This fact in itself is abundant testimony to the fundamental claim of *Jñāna-yoga* that ignorance (*avidyā*) is the source of ill-being of man, individually and collectively. Ill-being, then, can only be eliminated by eliminating ignorance; and ignorance can only be removed by knowledge (*jñāna*). Hence *Jñāna-yoga*, the Way of Knowledge.

Thus *Jñāna-yoga*'s answer to the question as to the status of God is as follows. The gods of various religions, including the so-called monotheistic ones, are not to be mistaken for ultimate reality, which alone is nameless and formless and hence inconceivable and indescribable. The various gods are *Saguṇa-Brahman*(s) as conceived of by different peoples. *Saguṇa-Brahman*, however, is not unreality; rather, it is an appearance, a phenomenon, and it is certainly efficacious in the development of religious consciousness toward the realization of ultimate reality. However, no conception of *Saguṇa-Brahman*, no matter how lofty and exalted, is to be identified with *Nirguṇa-Brahman*, the non-dual reality transcending all conceptions, low as well as high.

3. What, according to *Jñāna-yoga*, is the true being of man? We shall begin our answer by clearly distinguishing between ego — empirical, individual self — and *Ātman*, the Self. According to *Jñāna-yoga*, *Ātman*, the inmost Self of man, is pure, undifferentiated consciousness. Like the non-dual reality, also called *Brahman*, underlying the changing world of phenomena, *Ātman* is nameless and formless, and hence spaceless, timeless, imperceivable, unthinkable, and inexpressible. It is the unchanging, silent witness of the world of change and appearance. Like *Brahman*, *Ātman* transcends all distinctions. Consequently, it is reality, unsublatable by any other experience. Men in their ignorance mistakenly identify the *Ātman* with one or another of the appearances (names and forms), such as the body, the brain, the mind, etc. *Ātman* as reality is none of these things. Just as is the case with ultimate reality, *Ātman* cannot be experienced as an object in the world of appearances alongside other objects. On the contrary, it is the light which illuminates all objects — that which the eye cannot see but that by which the eye sees. One cannot doubt *Ātman* without falling into self-contradiction; that is, no one can consistently proclaim, "I am not conscious" In stark contrast, the individual self, the ego (*jīva*), is through and through phenomenal; and like all other phenomena, the ego is subject to change — arises and passes away. According to *Jñāna-yoga*, *jīva*, the empirical (phenomenal) self, is the appearance of *Ātman* under superimposition. We may introduce here Śaṅkara's concept of *upādhi*, meaning limitation, limiting adjunct. *Ātman*, which is infinite and eternal, appears to the ignorant as finite, time-bound *jīva* owing to the limiting conditions, physical as well as psychological, belonging in the realm of appearances. Thus, space, which is formless, one, and indivisible, assumes the form of the container, such as a vessel or a room. Similarly, *Ātman*, which is nameless, formless, eternal, and

infinite, appears as finite *jiva* owing to limitations such as the body and mind. It is due to ignorance (*avidyā*) that men identify themselves with one or another of the limiting conditions. But when one overcomes ignorance which manifests itself as superimposition and limitation, one knows the *Ātman* as the sole, unsublatable reality.

The chief aim of *Jñāna-yoga* is the conquest of this pervasive and deadening ignorance, ignorance as to the true being of man. The method, as by now should be clear to the reader, is systematic, rigourous, and unrelenting inquiry into the means of production of knowlege and the nature of knowledge so producible. It is thorough such inquiry that one comes to distinguish between the temporal and the finite and the time-bound on the one hand and the eternal and time-less on the other — that is, between appearance and reality. The insights one gains, through theoretical and experimental (phenomenological) pursuit of *Jñāna-yoga* result in one's discovery that the ego with which one identifies oneself is only an appearance (a phenomenon) and not reality. To say that the ego is merely an appearance is to say that the ego lacks own-existence and own-nature (*svabhāva-śūnya*). Thus, contrary to the chronically ignorant belief, the ego is impermanent and insubstantial. In a word, the ego is *empty*. Pain, sorrow, and suffering have their source in such ignorance. And it is an undeniable fact that human beings identify themselves, as a rule, with their bodies, minds, possessions, status, race, nationality, etc. But it is equally undeniable that all these things are bound to perish away sooner or later; and the mere thought of losing them is enough to bring one unspeakable pain and suffering. The point here is that it is due to ignorance that one identifies oneself with these things — ignorance as to the nature of phenomena as those which arise and pass away. *Jñāna-yoga* is the antidote to such ignorance, for *Jñāna-yoga* provides one with discriminating knowledge — *viveka-jñāna* — knowledge by which one discriminates between appearance and reality. On the dawning of such knowledge, one discovers one's true being to be the *Ātman* — objectless consciousness — which is at once the non-dual reality. This discovery is truely soteriological, in that one no longer identifies oneself with appearances. One is now wholly and for ever free of ignorance and hence of pain and suffering. For one with discriminating knowledge, death has lost its sting, since death can touch only appearances. Reposing in such knowledge, one lives in peace, joy, freedom, and wisdom.

Nothing could be a more fitting conclusion to this chapter than a brief description of the fourfold discipline (*sādhana-catuṣṭaya*), recommended by Śaṅkara as a practical aid to the aspirant. The discipline consists of *samanyāsa*, *śravaṇa*, *manana*, and *dhyāna*.

Samanyāsa consists in cultivating in oneself the following qualities: (a) the ability to discriminate between the real on the one hand and appearances and unreal on the other; the capacity to discern between the timeless and the time-bound, the eternal and the transient, the infinite and the finite; (b) total indifference to both pleasure and pain under all circumstances, either here or elsewhere; renunciation of all worldly desires and attachments; (c) tranquility, self-control, dispassion, fortitude, power of mental concentration, and faith in one's own ability to tread the path of knowledge; and (d) single-minded desire for true knowledge and freedom.

Śravaṇa is listening attentively to the wise and enlightened as they expound the great truths about man, the world, and reality as well as studying the works of the sages — for example, the *Upaniṣads* and the *Yoga-Sūtras*. Though *śravaṇa* one learns of the sole reality of *Brahman* and the identify of *Ātman* and *Brahman* (That thou art). In *śravaṇa*, the role of the *guru* (master) as a living example of the enlightened man cannot be overemphasized.

Manana is the state of reflection, in which the aspirant subjects to systematic analysis and investigation what he has learned from his teacher and the works of the sages. He examines the teachings and weighs them in the light of reason and experience — arguments, counter-arguments, analogies from everyday experience, facts of non-ordinary experience, etc. — and becomes convinced of their truth. But intellectual understanding and conviction alone, no matter how clear, firm, and convincing, can only provide mediate knowledge. Moreover, intellectual understanding and conviction are vulnerable, especially, under the burden of old habits of thought, resulting in the doubting and rejecting of what has hitherto been held as infallible truth. What is needed, then, is to transform the intellectually grasped mediate knowledge into one's own immediate experience. One therefore undertakes *dhyāna* (Yogic meditation) on the pivotal and liberating truth of *Jñāna-yoga*: the identity of the non-dual reality (*Brahman*) and pure — objectless — consciousness (*Ātman*). Through sustained intellectual inquiry and intense meditation, one comes to see in a flash of intuition — *prajñā* — that in one's true being one is indeed the sole reality.

Notes

1. Every act of reflexion is also an act of reflection, although not every act of reflection is necessarily one of reflexion; an act of reflection is also one of reflexion when the object of reflection is one's own mode of being.

2. Kant, *Critique of Pure Reason*, St. Martin's Press, New York, 1965, pp. 265, 266, 291, 382, 469, 471.

3. The terms 'monism' and 'non-dualism' are here used synonymously, although, strictly speaking, there is a fine difference between them: the former connotes unity and oneness and the latter simply non-duality and is preferred by *Jñāna-yogins* such as Nāgārjuna and Śaṅkara. But no harm is done in using them interchangeably, as long as one bears in mind the above distinction.

4. Patañjali's *Yoga-Sūtras* is the classic work on *Rāja-yoga*. There are innumerable translations and commentaries, ancient, modern, and contemporary, on this work; and among the best are: I. K. Taimni's *The Science of Yoga: A Commentary on the Yoga-Sūtras of Patañjali in the Light of Modern Thought*, Quest Books, Wheaton, Illinois, 1967; and *Yoga Philosophy of Patañjali*, by Swāmī Hariharānanda Āraṇya, with a foreword by Swāmī Gopilānanda, State University of New York Press, Albany, N. Y., 1983.

5. John C. Lilly, *Simulations of God*, Bantam Books, New York, 1976.

6. *See* F. Copleston, *A History of Philosophy*, 8 vols., Doubleday, Garden City, N. Y.

7. *The Philosophical Works of Descartes*, tr. by E.S. Haldane and G. R. T. Ross, Cambridge University Press, 1911, Meditation II, emphasis added.

8. William James, *Essays in Radical Empiricism and A Pluralistic Universe*, Longmans, Green & Co., New York, 1940, pp. 1-38.

4

Conclusion

In this last and final chapter, I shall draw together the salient points of this study. In addition, I shall make some observations which flow from the three fundamental principles of *Jñāna-yoga*, leaving it, in some cases, to the reader to see for himself the exact manner in which the observations follow as natural consequences of the principles.

(A) *Conclusions*: (1) The three fundamental principles of *Jñāna-yoga* are the following: (a) The Principle of Superimposition, (b) The Principle of Dependent Origination, and (c) The Principle of Two Truths. (2) According to the Principle of Superimposition, all expressible and communicable knowledge is the product of superimposing names and forms (concepts and percepts) on reality, which is itself nameless and formless. (3) It follows that the kind of knowledge a certain type of beings produce is inextricably bound up with their psycho-physiological makeup. (4) This in turn means that beings of different constitutions make different sets of knowledge-claims. In brief, all knowledge is species-bound and there can be no way of circumventing this truth. (5) A categorial framework consists of the various percepts, concepts, their definitions and the rules for their application, and methods and procedures by which to produce knowledge-claims as well as to certify their truth or falsity. This is the same as saying that every knowledge-claim is inseparably associated with some categorial framework or other. That is, there can be no such thing as an isolated knowledge-claim; rather, every knowledge-claim is relative to some categorial framework. (6) The categorial framework employed by a certain kind of being is only one among many within the range of potential for perception and conception of that kind of beings. It is precisely for this reason that we find among a given species of beings, say man, the employment of different categorial frameworks — for example, the Aristotelian, the Kantian, the Ptolemaic, the Copernican, the Newtonian, the Einsteinian, the Darwinian, etc. All these different frameworks lie within the range of potential for perception and conception of beings called 'human'. (7) It is due to ignorance of the fact that all knowledge-claims a given inquirer advances are ineluctably bound up with his own categorial framework that the thinker makes claims of absolute truth on behalf of his own knowledge-claims and dismisses those of others as false. In this manner arise dogmatism, intolerance, conflict, and opposition, which inevitably breed pain, sorrow, and suffering. (8) People uncritically and mistakenly believe that relative truths are falsehoods. It does not occur to them that to say that a given knowledge-claim is a relative truth is to say that the claim arises in a certain categorial framework and hence can only be certified through the percepts, concepts, definitions, rules, methods, and procedures of that framework. Underlying this erroneous belief — that relative truths are falsehoods — is the equally mistaken view that if a knowledge-claim is true it must be true, *simpliciter*, for all inquirers, irrespective of their psycho-physiological constitutions and hence of their frameworks. (9) Relative truth, contrary to ignorant and dogmatic views, is not a piece of falsehood; rather, it is truth which has its source in and is therefore certifiable through a certain categorial framework. It is thus sheer blindness and unwisdom to think that knowledge-claims are true (or false), independently of any and all categorial frameworks. (10) But what drives one to advance claims of absolute truth on behalf of one's own knowledge-claims? Answer: the thirst for knowledge of the absolute. This thirst for knowledge of the absolute and the unconditioned is at heart the quest for being. That is, since knowledge is a relation between the knower and the known, the knower, who initially encounters the world as the other, now tries to appropriate the world to himself through the knowledge he produces. But since the inquirer is wholly unaware of the means of production of knowledge and the nature of knowledge so produced, he uncritically and dogmatically goes on to claim absolute truth for his own knowledge-claims. Put pointedly, the inquirer has not conducted inquiry at Level 3, the flesh, blood, and bones of *Jñāna-yoga*. (11) Any claim to *describe* the real, the absolute, and the unconditioned is *necessarily* self-contradictory, and this is so according to none other than the percepts, concepts, definitions, and rules of the advocate's own categorial framework. What this goes to show is that the absolute and the unconditioned cannot be captured in any categorial framework — perceptual-conceptual network. This means that the absolute transcends all names and forms, and this is just the reason it cannot be described, and every purported description is therefore necessarily self-contradictory and absurd. (12) The absolute and the unconditioned, transcending all names and forms — concepts and percepts — is imperceivable, unthinkable, and inexpressible; for every perception, every thought, and every expression are inevitably bound up with some categorial framework or other. (13) This does not, however, mean that the absolute is beyond the pale of human experience; on the contrary, the real — the absolute — whose manifestations are the world of phenomena, under some superimposition, reveals itself when one brings about the cessation of all superimpositional activity; that is, upon the cessation of mental modifications. This is to say that the absolute is experienced neither perceptually nor conceptually, but rather in direct, non-perceptual, non-conceptual intuition — *prajñā*. It deserves to be emphasized that it is a pernicious error to think that the non-dual, ultimate reality and the world of phenomena are two numerically distinguishable ontological domains; quite the contrary, there is one, and only one, reality which, on the one hand, under superimpositional activity, is experienced by us as the world of phenomena, and, on the other, upon the cessation of superimpositional activity, is experienced as the non-dual, ultimate reality. Put another way, viewed through the veil of ignorance, reality appears to us as the world of phenomena; and upon the removal of the veil, reality is experienced as non-dual and ultimate, transcending space, time, names (concepts) and forms (percepts). Thus the passage from ignorance to enlightenment is not transportation from one ontological realm to another; rather, it is an epistemological transformation, transformation in the state of knowledge (*jñāna*). This is precisely what Nāgārjuna means when he teaches that there is not the slightest difference between *saṁsāra* (the world of phenomena) and *nirvāṇa* (ultimate reality). (14) But what does it mean to bring all superimpositional activity to a cessation? It means that the polar structure of ordinary experience — consciousness-versus-objects — collapses; upon such a collapse, the object pole, inevitably some phenomenon or other, of ordinary experience vanishes away, leaving pure, objectless consciousness as the ultimate residuum. Such consciousness is indeed the non-dual reality, beyond all categorial frameworks. (15) The Principle of Dependent Origination is the teaching that every phenomenon, without exception, arises and passes away in dependence upon other phenomena. Consequently, all phenomena are devoid of own-nature and own-existence; in a word, all phenomena are empty. (16) It has been shown that the statement of the Principle of Superimposition is the necessary condition for that of the Principle of Dependent Origination. (17) We have also displayed the projective relation between the two principles. (18) Just as the absolutization of a category leads to contradiction and absurdity, so also the absolutization of a phenomenon leads to contradiction — of regarding it as a non-phenomenon. The reason why no category can be absolutized without contradiction is that categories are relative and mutually dependent; and the reason why the absolutization of a phenomenon leads to contradiction is that every phenomenon arises and passes away in dependence upon other phenomena. (19) The thesis that all phenomena are relative is the same as the thesis that all phenomena are bereft of self-existence and self-nature, which in turn means that all phenomena are empty. (20) The Principle of Two Truths is the proclamation that knowledge and truth are of two kinds; the lower, relative, mundane, and conditioned on the one hand, and the higher non-relative, supramundane, and unconditioned on the other, respectively known as *saṁvṛtti* and *paramārtha*. Every lower truth is a perceptual-conceptual truth; in other words, every lower truth is a categorial truth (and hence cannot be absolutized without contradiction). In contrast, the higher truth is non-perceptual and non-conceptual — that is, non-categorial. For this reason, the higher truth transcends all categorial frameworks and can only be experienced in non-perceptual, non-conceptual, direct intuition (*prajñā*). (21) While in the case of every lower truth it is possible to distinguish between truth and being, no such distinction is possible with regard to the higher truth, since the higher truth is experienced precisely upon the collapse of the polar structure of ordinary experience. (22) Ultimate reality is Emptiness, Void (*śūnyatā*), in that it is neither a thing nor constituted of things. Another way of saying this is that ultimate reality is no-thingness (as contrasted with nothingness). (23) Just as there is *one* reality and *many* phenomena, so also there is *one* higher truth and *many* lower truths. (24) Upon the cessation of superimpositional activity, one experiences the non-dual reality; and since superimpositional activity is none other than mental modifications, the non-dual reality is one and the same as objectless consciousness, arising upon the cessation of mental modifications. The non-dual reality and objectless consciousness are known to the Upaniṣadic sages as *Brahman* and *Ātman*, respectively. It is this identity of *Ātman* and *Brahman* that is variously proclaimed in the Upaniṣadic teaching as, "I am *Brahman*", 'That thou art', *Prajñānam Brahma*, and *Ayam Ātma Brahma*, and so on. (25) The world of phenomena is neither real nor unreal; rather, it is an appearance and is therefore sublatable by reality, which alone is unsublatable. (26) Reality is unsublatable since there can be nothing besides reality by which it can be sublated. (27) Unreality is that which neither can nor cannot be sublated; the reason for this is two-fold: to say that unreality is sublatable is to imply that it is an appearance, whereas in fact unreality is that which cannot, in principle, be an object of our experience, actual or possible; on the other hand, to say that unreality is unsublatable is to imply that it is reality — a glaring contradiction. (28) Reality is unsublatable from the point of view of fact as well as that of value: from the point of view of fact it is unsublatable, because there can exist nothing besides reality by which to sublate it; and from the point of view of value reality is unsublatable, because there can be nothing of higher value and significance one may desire than the experience and knowledge of reality. (29) Theism, belief in a God who is the creator, protector, and destroyer of the universe, is not necessary at all for the pursuit of *Jñāna-yoga*; the reason for this is that the various gods of religions are only appearances — phenomena — and not reality, which alone is nameless and formless. The gods of different religions are none other than the products of our own senses, emotions, and intellect; as such, they are, unlike reality, describable and therefore sublatable. All these gods are *Saguna-Brahmans* (ultimate reality conceived of by different peoples as having qualities and relations), whereas there is only one reality, nameless and formless — *Nirguna-Brahman*. (30) It will be a mistake, however, to think that the gods of various religions are unreal, for they are all appearances and are undoubtedly efficacious in the development of religious consciousness toward the realization of ultimate reality. (31) No *Saguna-Brahman* (conception of ultimate reality), no matter how sublime and lofty, is to be mistaken for ultimate reality. (32) The ego (the empirical, individual self) is an appearance, since, like all other appearances, it arises and passes away. This is to say that the ego, like all other phenomena, lacks own-existence and own-nature; in brief, the ego is impermanent, insubstantial, and empty. (33) But, owing to ignorance (*avidyā*) as to his true being, man identifies himself with the ego or some aspect thereof, such as body, brain, mind, possessions, status, etc. And since all these things perish away sooner or later, pain, sorrow, and suffering are the ineluctable result of such identification; for is it not true that the mere thought of losing these things is enough to produce in one acute anxiety, fear, and suffering? (34) Thus it is ignorance of his true being that is the source of man's suffering. (35) According to *Jñāna-yoga*, man can overcome fear, pain, and suffering by overcoming the ignorance. (36) But how does one overcome ignorance? One conquers ignorance by discriminating knowledge (*viveka-jñāna*) resulting from the pursuit of *Jñāna-yoga*. Such knowledge enables one to clearly distinguish between appearances and reality, the time-bound and the timeless, the perishable and the imperishable. Armed with discriminating knowledge, one no longer identifies oneself with any appearances. Having discovered one's true being to be the eternal and immortal *Ātman* — pure consciousness, the non-dual reality — one lives in peace, joy, harmony, freedom, and wisdom. (37) *Jñāna-yoga*, in contrast to many philosophies, is not a mere logico-analytic inquiry; rather, it contains as an integral component phenomenological-experimental investigation, the methods and techniques of which are drawn from *Rāja-yoga*. The theoretical part of *Jñāna-yoga* is thus firmly grounded in our experiential base. For this reason, no critical examination and evaluation of *Jñāna-yoga* is possible without experimental inquiry. (38) *Jñāna-yoga* is not averse to rational-scientific inquiries — inquiries at Level 1 and Level 2. It has nothing to fear from these pursuits since it clearly assigns them their rightful place, the domain of lower truths. Thus, instead of fearing, belittling, and denigrating science, as most philosophies and religions do, *Jñāna-yoga* regards science, like art, as glowing testimony to the creativity of the human spirit. (39) *Paramārtha* — at once ultimate reality and the higher truth — itself not being a view (theory), is in full harmony with all views. This in turn means that conflict and opposition can only arise between one view of reality and another, but not between reality and any view whatever. (40) Failure to distinguish between reality and *views of* reality is the source of dogmatism and intolerance and therewith pain and suffering. Enamored of one's own view of reality, one identifies oneself with it and deems any criticism of the view as an attack upon oneself. (41) It is only of views of reality that one can properly speak of as being rational or irrational; and since reality transcends all views, reality is neither rational nor irrational, but rather non-rational. In a word, reality simply is. (42) *Jñāna-yoga* is one of the four paths to self-knowledge and knowledge of ultimate reality, and it is best suited to those who are predominantly of an inquiring bent. It is therefore imperative, before embarking upon the pursuit of *Jñāna-yoga*, that one find out whether this is the appropriate and efficacious path for oneself. For to follow a path that does not suit one well will not only be not beneficial to one but even harmful. 43. The crowning truth of *Jñāna-yoga* is the declaration of the identity of ultimate reality — the non-dual reality — and pure, objectless consciousness. Each of us has to determine for himself or herself the truth of this glorious declaration by meditating upon consciousness and discovering it to be the Emptiness (*śūnyatā*), nameless, formless, and non-dual.

(B) *Observations*: (1) All epistemology, theory of knowledge, is transcendentally grounded. How so? Since epistemology is inquiry into our ways of knowing, the inquiry cannot get off the ground unless one acknowledges *that one knows*. That is, "I know that I know" is the necessary condition for the possibility of epistemological inquiry. The point here is that knowing that one knows is wholly non-sensory — that is, it does not involve the instrumentality of the senses, and that is just what is meant by "transcendentally grounded". (2) There can be no such thing as an all-encompassing categorial framework. The reason for this is that every categorial framework, by its very nature, necessarily includes under itself certain percepts and concepts and excludes others. This follows directly from the polar character of all categories. (3) Many people, especially scientists and the so- called scientific philosophers, talk about theories *approximating* reality, or one theory approximating reality more closely than another. Let it be noted that any talk of approximation is intelligible only when one knows that of which something else is claimed to be an approximation. For is it not true that of a number of photographs we can say that one resembles a certain person more closely than the others only if we have seen that person at least once? And it is an undeniable fact that, as far as categorial knowledge is concerned (and scientific theories are categorial knowledge), one does not and cannot know reality apart from some theory or other. If so, what sense does it make to claim that one theory approximates reality more closely than another? None whatever. Furthermore, if one knows what reality is apart from theories — categorial frameworks — where is the need to construct theories, except perhaps as an idle pastime? The answer, again, is: none whatever. It is, however, perfectly sensible to talk about one theory as being pragmatically more efficacious than another. What this means, then, is that pragmatic efficacy is not to be mistaken for measure of approximation to reality. These observations follow from the impossibility of transcendental deductions of categorial frameworks. (4) Monism cannot, in principle, be *empirically* demonstrated. Reason? Monism is the thesis that the variety and multiplicity of existence is at bottom some single reality, be it matter, mind spirit, etc. This thesis cannot be empirically demonstrated, because all demonstration implies duality. Let us illustrate this point. Some people claim that colors are no more and no less than electromagnetic waves. But this view is clearly mistaken, for there are things which we can correctly say of colors but cannot sensibly say of electromagnetic waves. Furthermore, unless there is first the experience of colors, there can be no talk of reducing them to electromagnetic waves. Do we no longer experience colors after we have learned electromagnetic theory? Similar is the case with respect to the various monistic theories. Take, for instance, the claim that mind — the mental — is no more and no less than brain-processes. Unless one initially acknowledges the mental, for example thoughts, there can be no claim that thoughts are nothing but — one and the same as — brain-processes. What is more, the advocate of the thesis, like everybody else, continues to experience thoughts as thoughts and not as brain-processes. Most significant is the fact that there can be no talk of brain-processes if there is no thought; for the concept of 'brain-process' is not given to us by bran-processes but by thought. All this is a consequence of the fact that 'identity' is a transcendental concept, and not an empirical one. This means that all talk of identity in the empirical — phenomenonal — world necessarily implies distinguishability and hence of plurality. It is of course trivially true that the concept of self-identity holds empirically as well as transcendentally. We therefore conclude that identity, in the sense that all things are one, of the same reality, holds only transcendentally and never empirically. (5) It is an ancient and pervasive belief that God created the world out of nothing — creation *ex nihilo*. This view is clearly irrational and hence mistaken, unless one thinks of God as a cheap stage-magician who pulls rabbits out of an empty hat. Let us examine the issue closely. We are first told that prior to the creation of the world God alone is. That is, there was nothing besides God out of which to create the world. And it is one of the highest principles of rationality that nothing can be created out of nothing. This in turn means that God did not create the world but rather God *became* the world. In other words, God transformed Himself (Herself?) into the world. In this manner, all existence, including the allegedly lowliest and most insignificant, is God Itself. Seen in this way, divinity, sacredness, and holiness are not something that belong to a God who conceals Himself somewhere beyond the cosmos; quite the contrary, the entire world is holy, divine, and sacred. It is to be noted that this argument meets the highest criteria of rationality, and for him who understands it, the world is a spectacle of wonder, mystery, and holiness itself. (6) It is a widespread belief among those who consider themselves pious and religious that God created the world for some purpose (have we not heard the preachers, electronic and otherwise, constantly talk of God's plan?). These people are unaware that purpose can only be where there is duality; and since, prior to His becoming the world, God alone is, God could not have had any purposes. Further, since God is also construed as perfect, it is manifestly absurd and irrational to think that God has purposes, for purpose implies want, desire, and lack for the fulfilment of which one does something. It is also important to note that only machines are created to serve as means for the realization of some purpose or other. So all those who mistakenly think that God created the world for some purpose should really be thankful to God for not having had any purpose in creating the world; for had He created the world for some purpose, we would have been machines, and we know we are not. If you are still unconvinced, try, as you may, to think of yourself or your lover as a machine and see whether you succeed. (7) It is one of the greatest ironies that those who think of themselves as very scientific and rational deny mind and claim matter — the physical — as the sole reality. What is the irony here? The irony is that these people, if any, should be aware that science and the products of science are constructions of the mind. Thus Newton did not chance upon the great *Principia* while rummaging through some old English castle; rather, it is a product of his intellect; consequently, everything that results from the *Principia*, whether a rocket or the prediction of an eclipse, also bears the stamp of Newton's intellect. Or consider another example. Not long ago, there was, for instance, neither television nor supersonic aircraft. How did they come about? It is surely preposterous to suggest that people stumbled upon these things while wondering through the swamps of Georgia, the rainforest of Congo, or some prehistoric caves. What does this mean? It means that these objects are the products of human intellect; they are shining testimony to the creativity of the human spirit. Is it not a tragic irony, then, that the people who create these things should deny the reality of the very means by which they create them? (8) There are many, especially in Western societies, who, dazzled by the successes of science and awed by the prestige of scientists, think of God as a super scientist, in particular, a mathematical physicist, and believe that they thereby do honor to God. To think so, however, is to dishonor God. Let us ask: What exactly is it to do science? To do science is to produce knowledge of things not yet known on the basis of knowledge of things known, through hypothesis, theory, inference, experimentation, etc. This means that ignorance is a necessary condition for doing science. But if God is thought of as omniscient, where is the need for him to do science? Being omniscient, God knows all things at all places and times, past, present, and future, immediately, without the need for theory, inference, and so on. Thus God has no need for science; therefore, to think of God as a scientist, no matter how great, is to dishonor Him. (9) To mistake a lower truth for the higher truth has tragic consequences. Thus consider the unabated controversy between Biblical creationism and Darwinism. Is there really a conflict between the two? According to *Jñāna-yoga*, there is (and can be) no conflict or opposition between them. The defender of Biblical creationism is either unaware of or dogmatically dismisses the fact of the existence of a variety of creation-stories found in different cultures and societies. What this means is that all creation-stories are lower truths — imaginative accounts of how the world and the various beings in it came about. But out of ignorance one attaches oneself to the creation-accounts of one's own culture as the absolute truth and vehemently combats other accounts. The opposition between Biblical creationism and Darwinian theory is the result of such ignorance. Darwinian theory is but another account — an imaginative construction — of the panorama of life, and no one should claim absolute truth on its behalf. But, unfortunately, the so-called scientific biologists constantly pit Darwinism against Biblical creationism. Drawinian evolution is a scientific theory — view — and it will be retained as long as it enables us to successfully understand and manipulate the phenomenon of life; and when it is no longer successful, it will be rejected as inadequate for the purpose for which it was originally constructed. Just recall in the history of science how many theories had been so rejected and retired. Moreover, Drawinian theory, contrary to the charges of Biblical creationists, is concerned only with explaining how complex life-forms emerged from simpler ones, without the intervention of divine agency. Darwinian biology does not pretend to explain how the world came about, whereas Biblical creationism is an attempt to account for the very existence of the world. Many who claim to follow the teachings of Jesus never ask: if knowing the true and correct biological and astronomical theories is pivotal to attaining salvation, would a being as wise and compassionate as Jesus not have taught us the true and correct theories? Jesus did not exhort us to go to courts to defend Biblical creationism and Ptolemaic astronomy and fight tooth and nail Copernican and Darwinian theories; rather, his central exhortation is that we discover the kingdom of God *within ourselves*. How far is this exhortation from pitched legal battles about theories, one should judge for oneself. And it is a profound tragedy that one thinks one is following Jesus, while one is only busily and militantly combating Darwin or some other theorist. Such, then, are the gave consequences of mistaking a lower truth for the higher truth. There are innumerable myths and stories of creation and they are all lower truths; and to single out one's own lower truth and claim it as the higher truth — and there is only one — is a mark of ignorance and unwisdom. (10) What about the *problem of evil*? According to *Jñāna-yoga*, the existence of evil in the world is a problem only under certain assumptions. What are these assumptions? They are: (1) God is omniscient, (2) God is Omnipotent, (3) God is omnibenevolent, and (4) God created the world. Lucretius had long ago shown that, given the fact of evil, of the first three assumptions any two together are incompatible with the third. In any case, the following question naturally arises: If God is omnibenevolent, how could He have permitted evil in His creation? Theologians down through the ages wrestled with this problem and proposed various solutions. Some of these are as follows: Evil is not anything positive but is merely a privation (absence) of good; God permitted evil as training ground for the moral development of man; God is not responsible for evil, since He gave man freewill by which to choose and act; therefore, evil is the result of man's own wrong choices and actions; and so on. It is clear that the attempts to solve one problem — that of evil — only gave rise to another equally recalcitrant problem, that of freewill; and once again philosophers and theologians offered several solutions. What went wrong in all this? According to *Jñāna-yoga*, the problem of evil has its roots in man's ignorance (*avidyā*). What does this ignorance consist of? It consists of in the failure to distinguish between lower truths and the higher truth. That God is omnibenevolent is a lower truth, just as the claims of some people that God is jealous, that God is just, that God is wrathful, etc. Why are these lower truths? Because they are all merely various *conceptions* (views) of ultimate reality, not ultimate reality itself. That is, all these views pertain to *Saguṇa-Brahman*, and not to *Nirguṇa-Brahman*, which transcends all views, conceptions, and characterizations. Thus the existence of evil becomes a problem as a result of our own conceptions of ultimate reality. Once one realizes this, evil ceases to be a problem.

One might now ask: Are you denying there is evil in the world? And if you do not, how do you account for evil? The answers of *Jñāna-yoga* are as follows: Good and evil are polar and relative; this means that each exists in dependence upon the other. Here a word of clarification is in order. Contrary to popular but uncritical belief, the concepts 'polarily' and 'contradiction' are not synonymous. Contradiction pertains to thought, while polarity pertains to thought *and* being. Let us illustrate this point. Consider the mountain and the valley. They do not contradict each other; they exist simultaneously, not as a matter of chance and coincidence, but rather necessarily, the necessity being none other than polarity — which is not to be mistaken for *logical* necessity. What this means is that there *cannot* be a mountain without a valley, and *vice versa*; the existence of the one, instead of opposing that of the other (or rendering the other non-existent), depends upon the existence of the other. This is in keen contrast to contradiction; two statements are said to contradict each other, provided the truth of the one renders the other false, and *vice versa*. Thus, to say that two statements are contradictory is to say that not both can be true and not both can be false, whereas two things — phenomena — are polar provided both exist simultaneously or neither exists. The mountain does not contradict the valley anymore than the valley does the mountain. The coming into being of the mountain is at once that of the valley. It is only of our thoughts (and hence statements) about things that we can properly say that they are consistent with each other or contradict each other.

Now to say that good and evil are polar is to say that one cannot be without the other. It is the polar tension between good and evil that manifests itself as good on the one hand and evil on the other. If, per hypothesis, there is no evil, then there is no good either, and *vice versa*. What all this means is that if there is no good in the world, then there will necessarily — polar necessity — be no evil in it either, and *vice versa*. This is in full accord with the insight of *Jñāna-yoga* that the world of phenomena is through and through dualistic; it goes without saying that good and evil are relative, there being no such thing as good in itself (absolute good) or evil in itself (absolute evil). To take an example, it is a general belief that life is good and death is evil. But is it good to prolong a person's life, in spite of unbearable suffering due to an incurable illness? Is it not good to put an end to his suffering by letting him die, especially if the person prefers dying to living in excruciating pain, without any hope of cure? Only the ignorant, the dogmatic, the insensitive, and the inhumane think that death (or anything else, for that matter) is evil under any and all circumstances and hence should be prevented at any cost.

It is owing to ignorance of the polar nature of good and evil — nay, of all existence — that men have always labored under the most pernicious of illusions that an all-good world can be realized by eradicating evil. Think of the litany of horrors and the incalculable pain, misery, and suffering inflicted by man upon his fellowmen in his zealous attempts to implement his own blueprint of a vision (or lack thereof) which he is convinced will extirpate evil in the world and turn it into a paradise, you will see the point.

The goal and duty of all human beings of goodwill and wisdom, then, is not the elimination of evil in the world, but rather the minimization of evil. Given the polar character of evil, it simply cannot be eliminated. Thus the problem is not the existence of evil, but one of understanding how evil became a problem through our own ignorance — ignorance as to the polar tension that is existence itself and ignorance as to the distinction between lower truths and the higher truth. (11) Mind is the essence of time; that is, where there is no mind (mental modifications) there can be no sense of time. The truth of this claim is certifiable through sensory-deprivation experiments, in which the subject is placed in an environment so constructed that he receives no stimuli from it; in other words, the subject is in equilibrium with his environment. The significant point here is that, in spite of the absence of any stimuli from his environment, the subject will have a sense of time as long as thoughts and feelings arise and pass away. Thus it is the subject's awareness of the arising and passing away of thoughts and feeelings, *one after another*, that constitutes the sense of time. This is precisely what is meant by the claim of *Jñāna-yoga* that time has its source in mind (mental modifications). It now follows that all sense of time ceases upon the cessation of mental modifications. Thus, contrary to the so-called scientific claim that time has its basis in the external world, mind is the fountainhead of time. (12) The universe is intelligent. How so? If by 'universe' is meant the totality of existence (nothing can exist besides the universe), any intelligence one finds in the universe can only be due to the intelligence of the universe itself (for there can be nothing else to which it can be traced). And since everyone claims himself to be intelligent, the following inference is correct: "I, at least one being in the universe, am intelligent; therefore, the universe is intelligent." Note that for this inference to hold it is not necessary that *everything* in the universe be intelligent; for even if there is a single being that is intelligent, its intelligence can only be due to the intelligence of the universe. What this means is that, in keen opposition to the ignorant belief that the universe is dumb and unintelligent, it is the very source of all intelligence. But why do people think that they are intelligent but the universe is not? Answer: Since one talks about oneself on the one hand and about the universe on the other, one thereby mistakenly thinks that one is apart from the universe; one is unaware that the distinction one draws between oneself and the universe — subject-object distinction — is a distinction needed for the production of lower knowledge and does not mean that one exists apart from the universe. One does not exist apart from the universe; we have no being apart from the being of the universe. Hence no one can rationally (consistently) claim to be intelligent without at once acknowledging the intelligence of the universe. (13) The pivotal insight of *Jñāna-yoga* that in our true being we are objectless consciousness (the non-dual, ultimate reality) has profound consequences to psychology and psychotherapy. Ignorance of the teaching of *Jñāna-yoga* is responsible for the muddled and chaotic state of prevailing psychologies and therapeutic systems:

> . . . Our psychological theories are clumsy and inherently contradictory because we have misunderstood the observing center, the ground of our experience [objectless consciousness]. As a result of disregarding the unique character, the transcendent nature of that observing self, contemporary psychology has been unable to free us from the confinement of our isolating and improverishing assumptions.[1]

The above are some of the consequences of the tenets of *Jñāna-yoga*, and by no means do I claim that this list of observations is exhaustive. What is important is that each inquirer discover the power and fecundity of the Way of Knowledge by himself or herself traversing the path. Nothing less will do.

I shall leave the reader with one final thought: that we are conscious beings is an unparalleled mystery, a mystery far greater than the universe itself. For is it not true that consciousness — so near and yet so far — is the fulcrum on which turns all talk of the universe and countless beings therein? For this reason alone, it deserves the deepest of our meditations.

Note

1.   Arthur J. Deikman, *The Observing Self: Mysticism and Psychotherapy*, Beacon Press, Boston, MA., 1982.

Bibliography

Apte, V.M. (tr.), *Brahma-Sūtra-Śaṅkara-Bhāṣya*, Bombay, India: Popular Books, 1960.

Atreya, V.L., *The Philosophy of the Yoga-Vāsiṣṭha*, Adyar, Madras, India: The Theosophical Publishing House, 1936; *The Yoga-Vāsiṣṭha and Its Philosophy*, Varanasi, India: 1939.

Beardsley, Monroe (ed.), *The European Philosophers from Descartes to Nietzsche*, New York: Random House, 1960.

Blofeld, John (tr.), *The Zen Teaching of Huang Po*, New York: Grove Press, 1958; *The Zen Teaching of Hui Hai*, New York: Grove Press, 1970.

Bohm, David, *Wholeness and Implicate Order*, London: Routledge & Kegan Paul, 1981.

Briggs, John P. and F. David Peat, *Looking Glass Universe: The Emerging Science of Wholeness*, New York: Simon & Schuster, 1984.

Broad, C.D., *The Mind and Its Place in Nature*, Patterson, New Jersey: Humanities Press, 1960.

Brown, Harold, *Perception, Theory and Commitment: The New Philosophy of Science*, Chicago: The University of Chicago Press, 1977.

Buddhaghosha, *Visuddhimarga*, tr. by Bhikku Nyanamoli, *Path of Purity*, 2 vols., Berkeley, CA: Shambhala, 1976.

Capra, F., *The Tao of Physics*, Berkeley, CA: Shambhala, 1975.

Chang, Garma, *The Buddhist Teaching of Totality: The Philosophy* ˇ
    of Hwa Yen Buddhism, University Park, Pennsylvania:
    The Pennsylvania State University Press, 1974.

Churchland, Paul M., *Matter and Consciousness*, Cambridge,
    Massachusetts: The MIT Press, 1984.

Copleston, F., *A History of Philosophy*, 8 vols., Garden City, N.Y.:
    Doubleday.

Das, Rasvihary, *Introduction to Shankara: Being parts of Shankara's*
    commentary on the Brahma Sūtras rendered freely into English,
    Calcutta, India: Firma K.L. Mukhopadhyay, 1968.

Dasgupta, S.N., *A History of Indian Philosophy*, 5 vols., Delhi,
    India: Motilal Banarsidass, 1975.

Date, Vinayak Hari, *Vedānta Explained: Śaṁkara's Commentary on*
    the Bādarāyaṇa-sūtras, 2 vols., Bombay, India: Bookseller's
    Publishing Co., 1947.

David-Neel, Alexandra, and Lama Yongden, *The Secret Oral*
    Teachings in Tibetan Buddhist Sects, tr. by H.N.M. Hardy,
    San Francisco: City Lights, 1967.

Davies, Paul, *The Runaway Universe*, New York: Harper & Row,
    1978; *Other Worlds: A Portrait of Nature in Rebellion*, New
    York: Simon and Schuster, 1980; *The Edige of Infinity:*
    Where the Universe came from and how It will end, Simon
    and Schuster, 1981.

Deikman, A.J., *The Observing Self: Mysticism and Psychotherapy*,
    Boston: Beacon Press, 1982.

Dennett, Daniel C., *Brainstorms: Philosophical Eassays on Mind*
    and Psychology, Bradford Books, 1978.

de Reincourt, *The Eye of Shiva*, New York: William Morrow, 1981.

Deussen, Paul, *The System of the Vedānta*, tr. by Charles Johnston,
    New York: Dover, 1975; *The Philosophy of the Upanishads*,
    tr. by A.S. Geden, New York: Dover, 1966.

Deutsch, Eliot, *Advaita-Vedānta: A Philosophical Reconstruction*, Honolulu, Hawaii: East-West Center Press, 1969.

Edgerton, F., *The Bhagavad-Gītā: Translated and Interpreted*, Cambridge, MA: Harvard Oriental Series, 1944.

Edwards, Paul (ed.), *Encylopedia of Philosophy*, 8 vols. New York: Macmillan, 1967.

Eliade, Mircea, *Patañjali and Yoga*, tr. by Charles Markmann, New York: Funk and Wagnalls, 1969; *Yoga, Immortality and Freedom*, Princeton, New Jersey: Princeton University Press, 1971.

Evans, C.O., *The Subject of Consciousness*, New York: Humanities Press, 1978.

Farber, Marvin, *The Foundation of Phenomenology*, Albany, N. Y.: State University of New York Press, 1967.

Feurstein, G., *The Essence of Yoga*, New York: Grove Press, 1974.

Feyerabend, Paul K., *Against Method*, New York: Schoken Books, 1978; *Science in a Free Society*, Schoken Books, 1979.

Fingerette, H., *The Self in Transformation*, New York: Harper & Row, 1963.

Gale, George, *Theory of Science*, New York: McGraw-Hill, 1979.

Harre, Rom, *The Principles of Scientific Thinking*, Chicago: The University of Chicago Press, 1970.

Heidegger, M., *Discourse on Thinking*, tr. by John M. Anderson and E. Hans Freund, New York: Harper & Row, 1966.

Hopkins, J. and Lati Rimpoche (tr.), *The Precious Garland & The Song of the Four Mindfulnesses: Nāgārjuna and Kaysang Gyatso*, New York: Harper & Row, 1975.

Huxley, Aldous, *The Perennial Philosophy*, New York: Harper & Row, 1970.

Inada, K., *Nagarjuna: A Translation of his Mūla-madhyamaka-*

kārikā, with an Introductory Essay, Tokyo, Japan: Hokuseido Press, 1970.

James, William, *Radical Empiricism and A Pluralistic Universe*, New York: Longmans, Green & Co., 1943; *The Principles of Psychology*, 2 vols., New York: Dover, 1950.

Johnston, Charles (tr.), *The Yogasūtras of Patañjali*, London: Stuart and Watkins, 1970.

Jones, Roger, *Physics as Metaphor*, Minneapolis, Minnesota: University of Minnesota Press, 1982.

Kaltermark, Max, *Lao Tzu and Taoism*, tr. from French by Roger Greaves, Stanford, CA: Stanford University Press, 1969.

Kant, Immanuel, *Critique of Pure Reason*, tr. by N.K. Smith, New York: St. Martin's Press, 1965.

Kockelmans, J.J. (ed.), *Phenomenology: The Philosophy of Edmund Husserl and Its Interpretation*, Garden City, N.Y.: 1967.

Körner, Stephan, *Categorial Frameworks*, New York: Barnes & Noble, 1972.

Kuhn, Thomas S., *The Structure of Scientific Revolutions*, 2nd edn., Chicago: The University of Chicago Press, 1970.

Kupperman, J.J., *Philosophy: The Fundamental Problems*, New York: St. Martin's Press, 1977.

Lama Govinda, *Creative Meditation and Multi-dimensional Consciousness*, Wheaton, Illinois: Quest Books, 1976.

Lilly, John C., *Simulations of God*, New York: Bantam Books, 1976.

Mahadevan, T.M.P., *The Philosophy of Advaita*, London: Luzac & Co., 1938.

McCormick, P. and Elliston, F. (ed.), *Husserl: Shorter Works*, Notre Dame, Indiana: University of Notre Dame Press, 1981.

Merrell-Wolff, Franklin, *Pathways Through to Space*, New York: Julian Press, 1973; *The Philosophy of Consciousness without-an-object*, New York: Julian Press, 1973.

Moon, Ralph and Randall, Stephen (ed.), *Dimensions of Thought: Current Explorations in Time, Space and Knowledge*, 2 vols., Emeryville, CA: Dharma Publishing, 1980.

Munevar, G., *Radical Knowledge: A Philosophical Inquiry into the Nature and Limits of Science*, Indianapolis, Indiana: Hackett, 1981.

Murti, T.R.V., *The Central Philosophy of Buddhism: A Study of the Madhyamika System*, London: Allen & Unwin, 1960.

Muses, Charles and Young, A.M. (ed.), *Consciousness and Reality: The Human Pivot Point*, New York: Discus Books, 1974.

Nāgārjuna and Lama Mipham, *Golden Zephyr: Instructions from a Spiritual Friend*, tr. by Leslie Kawamura, Emeryville, CA: Dharma Publishing, 1975.

Pearce, Norman, *Space, Time, and Self*, Wheaton, Illinois: Quest Books, 1971.

Pelletier, K.R., and Garfield, Charles, *Consciousness: East and West*, New York: Harper & Row, 1976.

Prem, Sri Krishna, *The Yoga of the Bhagavad-Gītā*, Baltimore, Maryland, Penguin Books, 1973.

Puligandla, R., *Fundamentals of Indian Philosophy*, New Delhi; D.K. Printworld, 1997; *An Encounter with Awareness*, Wheaton, Illinois: Quest Books, 1981.

Radhakrishnan, S., *The Bhagavad-Gītā: Translation and Commentary*, London: Allen & Unwin, 1950; *The Brahmasutra: The Philosophy of Spiritual Life* (Translation with an Introduction and Notes), New Yoek: Greenwood Press, 1968; *The Philosophy of the Upanishads*, London: Allen & Unwin, 1935; *The Principal Upanishads*, London: Allen & Unwin, 1953.

Radhakrishnan, S. and Charles A. Moore (ed.), *A Sourcebook in Indian Philosophy*, Princeton, New Jersey: Princeton University Press, 1967.

Ramanan, K.V., *Nāgārjuna's Philosophy: As Presented in the Mahā-Prajñāpāramitrā-Śāstra*, Varanasi, India: Bharatiya Vidya Prakashan, 1971.

Reiker, Hans-Ulrich, *Hatha Yoga Pradipika: The Yoga of Light*, tr. by Elsy Bechrer, Middletown, CA: The Dawn Horse Press, 1971.

Rogo, D. Scott, *Parapsychology: A Century of Inquiry*, New York: Dell Publishing, 1975.

Rucker, Rudy, *Infinity and the Mind*, Boston: Birkhauser, 1982.

Sastry, A. Mahadeva (tr.), *The Bhagavad-Gītā, With the Commentary of Śaṅkarācārya*, Madras, India: Ramaswamy Sastrulu & Sons, 1961.

Schrödinger, E., *What is Life and Other Essays*, Garden City, N.Y.: Doubleday, 1956.

Schumann, H.W., *Buddhism: An Outline of its Teachings and Schools*, Wheaton, Illinois: Quest Books, 1973.

Sheldrake, R., *A New Science of Life: The Hypothesis of Formative Causation*, Los Angeles, CA: J.P. Tarcher, Inc., 1981.

Singh, Jaideva, *Introduction to Madhyamaka Buddhism*, Varanasi, India: Bharatiya Vidya Prakashan, 1968.

Singh, Ram Pratap, *The Vedānta of Śaṁkara: A Metaphysics of Value*, Jaipur, India: Bharat Publishing House, 1949.

Snyder, Paul, *Toward One Science*, New York: St. Martin's Press, 1978.

Sprung, Mervin (ed.), *The Problem of Two Truths in Buddhism and Vedānta*, Dordrecht, Holland: Reidel, 1973.

Stace, W.T., *The Teachings of the Mystics*, New York: Mentor, 1960.

Suzuki, E.T. (tr.), *The Lankāvatāra Sūtra*, London: Routledge & Kegan Paul, 1930; *Studies in the Lankāvatāra Sūtra*, London: Routledge & Kegan Paul, 1975.

Swāmī, Mādhavānanda (tr.), *The Bṛhadāraṇyaka Upaniṣad, with the Commentary of Śaṅkarācārya*, Mayavati, Almora, India: 1950.

Swāmī, Nikhilānanda, *Self-Knowledge: An English Translation of Śaṅkarācārya's Ātmabodha*, Madras, India: Ramakrishna Math, 1947.

Swāmī, Prabhavānanda and Christopher Isherwood (tr.), *Śaṅkara's Crest-Jewel of Discrimination, with a Garland of Questions and Answers*, New York: Mentor, 1970; *The Song of God: Bhagavad-Gītā*, New York: 1951.

Swāmī, Prabhavānanda and F. Manchester (tr.), *The Upanishads: Breath of the Eternal*, New York: Mentor, 1957.

Swāmī, Venkateśwarānanda, *Yoga-Vāsiṣṭha* (translation with commentary), 2 vols., Chiltern Elgin, Cape Province, South Africa: Yoga Trust, 1976.

Taimni, I.K., *The Science of Yoga: A Commentary on the Yoga-sūtras of Patañjali in the light of Modern Thought*, Wheaton, Illinois: Quest Books, 1967.

Tart, Charles (ed.), *Transpersonal Psychologies*, New York: Harper & Row, 1975.

Thibaut, George (tr.), *The Vedānta Sūtras of Bādarāyaṇa, with the Commentary by Śaṅkara*, 2 vols., New York, Dover, 1970.

Turner, Merle B., *Philosophy and the Science of Behavior*, New York: Appleton-Century-Crofts, 1967.

Waley, Arthur, *The Way and Its Power: A Study of the Tao Te Ching and Its Place in Chinese Thought*, New York: Grove Press, 1958.

White, John (ed.), *The Highest State of Consciousness*, New York: Doubleday, 1975.

Whiteman, Michael, *Philosophy of Space and Time*, New York: Humanities Press, 1967.

Wilber, Ken (ed.), *Holographic Paradigm and other Paradoxes*, Boulder, Colorado: Shambhala, 1982; *Up From Eden*, Boulder, Colorado: Shambhala, 1981; *The Spectrum of Consciousness*, Wheaton, Illinois: Quest Books, 1977.

Wolman, Benjamin (ed.), *Handbook of Parapsychology*, New York: Van Nostrand, 1976.

Wood, Ernest, *The Glorious Presence: The Vedānta Philosophy, including Śankara's Ode to the South-facing Form*, Wheaton, Illinois: Quest Books, 1974; *Seven Schools of Yoga*, Wheaton, Illinois: Quest Books, 1973; *The Pinnacle of Indian Thought: verse-by-verse translation and commentary in the Vivekacūdāmani of Śrī Śankarācārya*, Wheaton, Illinois: Quest Books 1971.

Woodroffe, Sir John, *The World as Power*, Madras, India: Ganesh & Co., 1974.

Young, Arthur M., *Geometry of Meaning*, New York: Delacorte, 1976; *The Reflexive Universe: Evolution of Consciousness*, New York: Delacorte, 1976; *Which Way Out? and other Essays*, San Francisco, CA: Robert Briggs Associates, 1980.

Younger, Paul, *Introduction to Indian Religious Thought*, Philadelphia: The Westminster Press, 1971.

Zimmer, H., *Philosophies of India*, ed. by Joseph Campbell, Princeton, New Jersey: Princeton University Press, 1969.

Zukav, G., *The Dancing Wu-Li Masters: An Overview of Modern Physics*, New York: William Morrow, 1980.